GOOD HOUSEKEEPING
FAMILY LIBRARY

DOING UP
YOUR HOME

GOOD HOUSEKEEPING
FAMILY LIBRARY

DOING UP
YOUR HOME

Shirley Green

SPHERE BOOKS LIMITED
30-32 Grays Inn Road, London, WC1X 8JL

First published in Great Britain in 1973 by
Ebury Press
First Sphere Books edition 1975

© The National Magazine Co. Ltd. 1973

ISBN 0 7221 3952 7

Cover picture by Paul Redman

Filmsetting in Britain by
Typesetting Services Ltd, Glasgow.
Printed and bound in Belgium by
Henri Proost & Cie p.v.b.a., Turnhout.

CONTENTS

FOREWORD

Most people have a vision of the kind of home they would like to live in: a place which is not only lighter, roomier and more convenient than it is at present, but which has a special look and 'feel' that is essentially their own. The aim of this book is to help you turn the home you have into something closer to what you have in mind.

The rewards of doing up your home are both immediate and long term, but the actual process can be a long, hard haul. Shirley Green's advice will help you thread your way through the pitfalls and avoid the blunders that can be so costly. It will also save you weeks of hunting around; the notes to each chapter at the end of the book tell you exactly where to go for what.

Author and journalist, Shirley Green has an expert knowledge and much personal experience of doing up flats and houses. Readers of GOOD HOUSEKEEPING, of whose Homes Department she was formerly a member, will recognise in these pages the relaxed, unfussy grace that has come to be identified with the magazine.

If you feel that you would like individual expert advice on planning your colour schemes, the magazine runs a Colour Service of which you may like to avail yourself—particulars are given on page 138. The magazine's Furnishing Department also answers decoration queries of all kinds (a stamped addressed envelope should be enclosed) though, naturally, they cannot provide detailed schemes in the same way as the Colour Service. The address to write to is: GOOD HOUSEKEEPING, Chestergate House, Vauxhall Bridge Road, London SW1V 1HF.

Isabel Sutherland
General Editor
Good Housekeeping Family Library

Note: The section at the end of the book, *Notes to Chapters*, contains additional information concerning points raised in each chapter; references to these are given throughout the text in brackets. Thus (*5.2) refers to the notes to Chapter 5, point 2.

1 A HOME IS WHAT YOU MAKE IT

To begin at the beginning. Hardly any of us manage to buy the house of our dreams. We may want to live in an elegant Regency terrace—we can only afford a two-up-two-down in a mean Victorian row. We want to buy a tumbledown country cottage with bags of character—we can only get a mortgage on a faceless new redbrick bungalow. We may have visions of a spacious, avant garde architect-designed house but have to settle for one with the bay windows and leaded lights preferred by most building societies. Obviously financial limitations are something we have to accept; but we *don't* have to accept the limitations of the house itself (*1.1). Because once inside our own front doors—give or take a few building regulations outlined in Chapters 3 and 4—we can do whatever we like.

There's no law that says old houses have to be furnished with antiques or new ones with modern furniture. Nothing to say that town houses have to look cool and sophisticated and country cottages cosy and chintzy. Just a lot of pre-conceived notions that are best forgotten unless they happen to fit in with what you really want.

This doesn't mean you should ignore your basic house completely. Naturally, you'll need to be influenced by its mood and proportions; you'll have to treat it with sympathy and use its natural assets to best advantage. But there's a lot of difference between being influenced and being dictated to.

Take a country cottage for instance. Most people paint the walls and ceiling white and stain the beams a dark brown. They put pretty floral curtains at the windows, cover traditional armchairs with chintz or velvet, and if they can afford it, fill the rooms with antiques, oil paintings and Persian carpets. It's a cliché, but one that always works, automatically creating a mellow mood, and suggesting winter evenings round the inglenook.

But if you have a sunny, extrovert nature, there's no reason why you shouldn't throw off the cosy, almost claustrophobic image. Why not paint the walls a strong, punchy colour and pick out the beams in white? Why not put roller blinds at the windows—they're probably too tiny to take the clutter of curtains anyway? Or, if you're surrounded by acres of greenery that no one can see through, why not forget blinds altogether and simply paint the window reveals a bright colour to give them importance.

9

Preserving the character

Provided you keep the effect bold and simple, you'll still be in tune with the essential cottage character. But this does mean keeping the flooring basic—covering it with something like quarry tiles, or if that's too cold, tough sisal carpeting or rush matting. It means using furniture sparsely, so it makes a clear-cut statement instead of muddling happily into the background. (Whether it's antique, modern, or both, doesn't matter: the main thing is that it should be straightforward and unfussy.) It means using plenty of natural textures, whether you introduce them with rush-seated chairs, a scrubbed pine dresser or a wicker basket for keeping the logs in. It means having a definite

Typical country cottage gets an untypical treatment. Back door is painted a bold and uncompromising orange, a modern *Tomotom* chair punches home the colour impact, and the small windows don't even bother with roller blinds, let alone predictable chintz curtains. Simple approach, and natural textures like the exposed brickwork and rough sisal carpet, make sure the result stays sympathetically rustic.

colour scheme; not the usual pretty pastels that create a passive setting, but no-nonsense primary colours that make a positive contribution. And of course, it means keeping the bric-à-brac to a minimum, whether you go for brass warming-pans and copper kettles or Swedish glass and salt-glazed pottery.

Clichés become clichés *because* they work. It takes a lot of confidence to turn your back on them and risk something different. This is just as true if you move into a Georgian or Regency house, with lofty ceilings, beautifully-proportioned windows and an air of grandeur it's difficult to live up to. Of course, you may want to live up to it, with 18th century furniture, wall-to-wall carpeting and luxuriously-draped velvet curtains. And it'll look very elegant. But if you want

Cottage living room turns convention inside out by painting the beams white and 'the walls dark instead of the other way round; by whitewashing the fireplace instead of leaving it red brick; by putting a Mexican bark painting above it instead of a routine hunting print; by preferring a modern coffee-cum-storage table and chair to inevitable antiques. Again, the result's relaxed and natural.

Michael Boys

Paul Redman

Proof that a home is what you make it. Apart from the furniture and furnishings, this cool and aloof dining room is in fact the same as the warm and friendly one on the cover.

12

something friendlier (and less expensive), there's no reason why you shouldn't sand and seal the floorboards and forget about carpets; have good modern furniture or a mixture of old and new; cover the walls with something like hessian instead of 'Regency-striped' wallpaper; and if you're lucky enough to have the original shutters, you can make use of them in place of conventional curtains.

The Edwardian house shown on page 30 illustrates perfectly how you can pull a period home into the 1970s and still keep in sympathy with the basic structure. So does the Georgian house on page 44. It's every bit as grand as it must have been in its hey-day, but it's uncompromisingly modern, with off-white ceiling, walls, floors, window-blinds and furniture, long low sofas in chunky, squared-off shapes and vibrant-coloured cushions scattered about for impact.

What if you've moved into a 1970s house? If you like modern homes, you'll probably play the modernity up to the hilt, as in the dining room on page 12. But if you yearn for something more friendly and familiar, it's easy to take the same room and make it look lived-in and almost cottagey. First give it plenty of warm colours—say, sand on the walls and a rich tobacco brown on the floor. Then give it plenty of natural texture—make the carpet long-pile or twist-pile instead of smooth, close-pile Wilton. Add the warmth of wood, whether you buy a new pine chest, for instance, or refurbish an old one; if you run shelves along the wall, don't paint them, leave them natural. Pick pretty and un-pretentious things: cane dining chairs with an intricate pattern, a fabric that's modern but full of naive charm. It's perfectly possible to buy everything new and achieve a comfortable, thoroughly-established atmosphere. And if you don't believe us, take another look at the dining room on the cover. It's exactly the same as the one on page 12 except that its owner moved in with very different ideas.

Sophisticating your 'semi'

Moving into a 1930s 'semi' is enough to make anyone's ideas shrivel up on the spot. It *is* daunting to know all the neighbours have got floral carpet in the halls, three-piece suites in the living rooms, and dressing tables in the upstairs bay windows. But there's no reason why you shouldn't go out on a limb and create a very sophisticated interior with, say, bitter chocolate carpet in the hall and up the stairs (perhaps with off-white walls, plenty of modern prints, stainless steel spot-lights and, if you can afford it, some new, dead-simple banisters). With modern seating units in the living room, grouped into a square 'conversation' area, instead of set at an angle round a ghastly mottled fireplace. With built-in storage in your bedroom instead of the cumbersome and space-consuming wardrobe, chest of drawers, and dressing table trio. And with crisp roller blinds at the bay window instead of frilly, knickerbocker drapes.

It doesn't cost any more to stamp a home with your own personality. It just takes a bit more confidence. And by the time you've finished reading this book, you should have that in abundance.

2 THE LIFE YOU LIVE

The average family has 2·4 children and moves house every ten years. It all sounds so simple, except that behind those bald statistics lie enough complications to confuse a computer. Because the trouble with the 'average' family, of course, is that its needs keep changing. The 2·4 babies don't come at once and worse still, as far as a computer's concerned, they don't stay babies. They're inconsiderate enough to grow up and once they've all been given separate bedrooms, they probably pack their bags and make homes of their own elsewhere.

Not many houses can keep up with this continual state of flux. There's a limit to how much they can expand and contract—though considerably less of one if you can afford structural alterations, as we'll see in Chapter 3. This probably explains why most families move every ten years. But even within those ten years, the average home is going to see plenty of changes.

While the babies *are* babies, they may not cause too much upheaval (not in terms of the space they occupy, anyway). They can sleep in your bedroom for the first few months; most child-welfare experts agree, brothers and sisters can share a bedroom during the early years without incurring psychological disaster. But as soon as they start spreading their wings and expanding their egos at school, you'll have them whooping around the house as if it's one big playground. And unless you live in the country and can turn them loose without worrying, you'll probably cast your eyes to the loft, and start saving for a loft conversion that will give them an away-from-it-all playroom. Things won't get any better when they reach their moody and introverted teens. Then they'll be demanding private pads where they can entertain their friends, and heaven help you if you intrude—unless it's to bring cups of coffee, of course.

You can't win. Especially as, even if you *don't* have children, there's no guarantee that your needs are going to stay static. As you make more friends you'll want to put more of them up for the weekend or when they miss the last bus home. As you develop more interests, you could get absorbed in a hobby

Right: 1 Bedsitter demonstrates how easy it is to turn a bedroom into a self-respecting and private teenage pad. **2** 'Dining room' shows how you can spread into the hall if your living/dining room is bursting at the seams.

14

1

Sale, Stone & Senior: setting, Diana Austen

2

John Cook: setting, Diana Austen

15

that demands a room of its own. And *because* you don't have children, you can bet that if an elderly relation needs looking after, you'll be the ones expected to do it.

The fluid approach

The only way a house can keep pace with the life you lead is for you to take a fluid approach to it. Don't regard the estate agent's particulars as an immutable law. Just because he says the ground floor has a living room, dining room and kitchen, these rooms don't have to be used in that way. You may find it impossible to work in your tiny kitchen with a toddler literally at your apron strings (dangerous in any case when there are red hot elements and saucepans on the boil). The solution could be to knock down the wall and have an open plan kitchen-cum-dining room, with a counter top and stable door between. This way you can keep your infant out of the Hollandaise sauce but keep him in the conversation, at the same time watching to make sure he's not up to any mischief.

Alternatively, you may want to knock the living room and dining room into one big through room if they're both tiny. This gives a much more relaxed way of living (especially if you don't have central heating and can only afford to warm one room). Also you'll be able to have friends round in comfort, instead of wedging them into one minute living room so tightly that they have to sit to attention.

Or you may discover that the reason you always hum when you make the beds is because the upstairs rooms get all the sunlight—to say nothing of a decent view—while downstairs all you get is gloom, plus a view of the garage and the garden wall. Never mind if your neighbours have their bedrooms upstairs, so the sunlight gets wasted during the day and all they do is draw the curtains on the view at night. If you can possibly manage it (this will depend on how much it costs to switch your kitchen and bathroom around), turn your house upside down, live on the first floor and sleep on the ground floor.

Incidentally, if you're buying a new house and want to know which windows will get the sunlight: if it faces north, the front will get a clear even light—the kind artists like for their studios—but no sunshine. That comes pouring in the back windows, which is fine if the kitchen's there and you spend hours cooking and doing the washing-up; better still if you make the back room your living room, regardless of what the builders meant it for. If the house faces south, sunshine pours in the front windows but not the back ones. If it faces south-east or south-west, you get morning or afternoon sun in the front windows respectively; north-west or north-east, you get morning or afternoon sun in the back windows respectively. It's up to you to decide which rooms you spend what time in, and if at all feasible, arrange them accordingly.

Conflicting interests

However you arrange the house basically, the living room is where everyone's going to congregate in the evening and somehow you've got to cater for as many different interests as possible. You may want to sit in a good light to do some sewing. Your husband may want the light off to watch television. Your daughter may want to sit quietly and do some homework. Your son may want to play his latest LP at full blast. Accept you're never going to be able to keep everyone happy within the same four walls and see what you can manage outside them.

Is there somewhere quiet where the children can do their homework or get immersed in a hobby? The obvious place is up (or down as the case may be) in their own bedrooms, where all it takes is a couple of whitewood chests and a bridging top to provide a desk with plenty of drawer space. Or there's the dining room (provided you didn't combine it into your living room long before you had homework problems). This isn't so satisfactory, because children have to keep picking up their bits and pieces and can't claim the territory as their own, but it may have to do. And if you don't have a dining room, consider creating a working place in the hall. It may have room for a long, rectangular table and chairs—or simply a flap-down desk-top if you're really pushed for space. Or it may have space under the stairs that's going begging, now the prams and pushchairs have become obsolete. This can be fitted out to make a complete mini-study, with a deep work-top, drawers below (remember to leave room for legs, or it won't be very popular), shelves above, and an adjustable angle lamp fixed to the wall (spot-lights would get very hot in such a restricted area).

Of course, *none* of these suggestions are going to prove practicable unless you have central heating (*2.1). Failing this, there are bound to be wails of protest if you push kids out into an unheated part of the house; no one can *think* to do homework, let alone hold a pen, if they're stuck in some icy corner that's like being exiled to Siberia. In this respect, central heating really can be a form of economy. It means you can *use* every part of your house—and if you ever decide to move, you're sure to recoup at least the cost of installation in the selling price.

Creating separate areas

But back to the living room. Does it have to be dominated by the television? In most cases, the realistic answer is yes, because the majority of people want it that way. (If the answer is no, get a portable that can be carried to wherever it will create the least disturbance.) But even so, the room doesn't have to look like a cinema, with all the chairs lined up facing it and you appearing in the natural breaks with meals and cups of coffee like an usherette. Divide the room into separate areas—one for eating in if you don't have a separate dining room (with a pendant light-fitting that isolates the table-top in a pool of light and throws everything else, including the box which you *shouldn't* be watching at meal-times, into shadow). Then another area into one for sewing or reading (with a standard spot-light to throw a strong, self-contained light that won't interfere with television viewing). And make the television an integral part of the room, so it isn't the first thing that hits you in the face when you walk in. The simplest way is to incorporate it in a run of storage units. Then you can fill other shelves with plants, books and bric-à-brac, so it becomes part of an attractive and restful focal point, instead of something that demands attention even when it's switched off.

This is the best way to humanise the ugly clutter of hi-fi systems too. Break up the anonymous record-deck, amplifier and speaker components with plenty of personal paraphernalia. And solve the problem of how to

This open-plan kitchen and living area started life as a separate kitchen and morning room—all very well, except it was dangerous cooking with a tiny and bored toddler around. Solution was to knock both rooms into one (pine-boarded kitchen ceiling, an idea pinched from a local steak house, hides the steel joint that had to be put in), and now Mum can keep an eye on her daughter as she cooks. Room divider is simply a run of kitchen units, backed with blackboard to make a scribbling surface; white laminate breakfast bar folds down when not wanted.

19

listen to music while the television's on by buying a set of stereo headphones, so you can slide into a private world of sounds and not be a nuisance to anyone.

Make extensions self-contained

The snag about expanding your house to meet your family's needs is that unless you start looking after elderly parents, you only need it while the children are growing up. Once they've vanished for Marrakesh or marriage, you're left with a lot of rooms on your hand and nothing to do but go round and dust them. This is something to bear in mind before you extend your home in any way. Try to make any extra living space as easily accessible and self-contained as possible, so that if you want to, you can let it off at a later date. And if you're converting a basement or loft or adding an extension, try to incorporate a bathroom so you don't ever find yourself having to share the bath with strangers.

Obviously the ideal would be a completely self-contained flat, especially as if it's part of the original house, rather than a new extension, it will be eligible for a Discretionary Grant of up to £1,200. This way you could let it while you were newly married and hard up (furnished of course, or you'd never be able to get the tenants out), then reclaim it for yourself as the children came, and let it off again once they'd left home. But there's one major snag here. Most people buy their homes on a mortgage; you can't make any structural changes to it without building society approval; and building societies won't give permission for you to make a flat to let. In fact theoretically, you're not supposed to let out rooms at all—so we'd better not encourage you to break the rules!

3 SPACE FROM NOWHERE

Even the smallest house may have possibilities you haven't thought of. Are you *sure* you've used existing space to best advantage, or could you knock down a wall here, fit in an extra lavatory and wash basin there? And if it's bursting at the seams already, are you sure you can't make it bigger by going upwards with a loft conversion, downwards with a cellar conversion, or outwards with a house extension? All these drastic tactics are expensive— but every time a bill comes in, cheer yourself up with the thought that you're making an investment. If ever you come to sell your house, you should get all your money back, plus something extra to make the effort worthwhile.

Before you get carried away with enthusiasm, remember you can hardly wield a hammer in your own home without asking somebody else's permission. For a start, *is* it your own home? If it's leasehold (even if it's on a 999 year lease) you'll have to get the freeholder's agreement before you make any structural alterations. And even if it's freehold, if you've got a mortgage, you'll have to get permission from the mortgager, whether it's a building society, local authority, insurance company or bank. This may seem unfair, but obviously they want to be sure that your house is as good a selling proposition after you've had a go at it as before. This is just the beginning. Building Permission and Planning Permission (by no means the same thing: the Planning Department may say yes to your proposed loft conversion while the Building Department may say no, because you haven't provided strong enough floor joists) are something else again, and are dealt with later as they arise.

Can you do *anything* without getting permission from Uncle Tom Cobley and all? Well, you can rip out an old fireplace and block up the opening; though remember to incorporate a ventilation grill or your room will start getting stuffy. This won't make your room much bigger (though it could provide extra storage if you filled the opening with shelves instead of blocking it up; it could even accommodate that monster eye, the television, in a neat and discreet way). But if you want to put in a window or take one out, put in a door or take one out, you've got to go through the complete rigmarole of getting Building, and possibly Planning Permission—and just as well.

Bang a door or window opening into a load-bearing wall and you might get a much bigger opening than you bargained for!

Knocking down a wall

Converting two rooms into one doesn't actually create more space; it just seems to. If you live in an older house, and your hall is long, narrow and gloomy while the living room leading off it is light, bright but small, banging down the wall will give you one big, airy room; something that'll welcome guests instead of making them think they've come to a penitentiary. Similarly, if you live in a 1930s house or a workman's cottage, where your two ground floor reception rooms are too small to receive anyone but midgets, you may well want to knock down the dividing wall and have one spacious through-room with double the light.

This isn't something you need Planning Permission for. Planning Departments are only concerned if you want to change the *use* of the building (for example, if you wanted to make a self-contained flat in your home, where you'd be changing it from single occupation to multiple occupation) or if you want to change the outside appearance of the building (for example, if you wanted to replace a small, poky window with a large, picture version that would stand out like a sore thumb from similar houses in the street). But it *is* something you need Building Permission for—from the District Surveyor if you live in Inner London, or from the Building Inspector if you live outside London. This is because although many internal walls are merely partitions separating one room from another, others are load-bearing, and help hold up the rest of the house.

If it *is* a partition (and out of the kindness of his heart, the local Building Inspector or District Surveyor may come and tell you one way or another), you should be able to get the job done quite cheaply by a local builder as it will only be a matter of demolition and making good afterwards. But if you don't have obliging officials to advise you, *never* take the builder's word for it. He won't deliberately try to kill you but he probably won't be qualified to know whether what he's doing is safe or not; and he won't be so cheap when the Building Inspector finally arrives and says it's going to cost another £300 or more for a load-bearing steel beam to be inserted. Because that's what you're likely to need if you're proposing to sweep away the wall completely (though it might be cheaper to have functional pillars or simply make a double door through the room with a strong, supporting lintel above it). These aren't things you can expect the Building Inspector to tell you—he's there to make sure what you do is right—not tell you how to do it. What you need is an architect or building surveyor—and we'll go into how to find them and what they cost in the next chapter.

Taking pressure off the bathroom

Nothing makes a house seem smaller than the morning scrum to get into the one and only bathroom. If you haven't got room for a second bathroom, see if it's economically feasible to install a wash basin and/or shower cubicle

Jessica Strang

A gallery bedroom is only possible in a bed-sitter because of the Fire Regulations. But provided you comply with the Building Regulations, there's nothing to stop you making a gallery dining room above a living room—even a gallery kitchen if you can cope with the plumbing costs.

in any of the bedrooms. The problem here is plumbing. Unless the bedroom's near enough to the bathroom to share its waste pipes, you're going to get involved in ripping up floorboards, knocking holes in internal and external walls, and paying a bill so big it would have bought you a new car. Even so, plumbers' estimates are free, and you've nothing to lose by getting two or three.

A second lavatory is even more essential in a crowded house, especially as it can be kept neat and tidy so that visitors don't have to trip over the family's plastic ducks and submarines to reach it. Once again, plumbing's the big problem; unless your new soil pipe can connect to an existing drainage run and drain, you'll find yourself footing a hefty bill. But it's not your only problem, because lavatories are not allowed to open directly on to a habitable room or kitchen. (Bedrooms are an exception, provided the first lavatory in the house can be reached without passing through a bedroom, kitchen or habitable room). This means that unless your second lavatory leads off a hall or landing, it's going to necessitate the building of a small, transitional lobby—something that will take up valuable space you can ill afford. As if that isn't enough, there are very strict rules about ventilation. Ventilation to a room containing a lavatory must be direct to the outside air and cannot be through any other room or enclosure. In other words, a lavatory practically demands to be installed against an outside wall where you can put in a small window or ventilation grid. (Practically, because it *is* possible to run an air vent from the outside of the house into an internal lavatory, and ventilate it by a mechanical extractor fan, but the regulations are complicated and it does get expensive.)

Space under the stairs: Fortunately the picture isn't always as grim as the problems make it sound. In fact, if you live in a conventional semi-detached house, the solution could be staring you right in the face. Most of these share a common living room wall, so that one big chimney breast can make do for both houses. This means the hall and stairs are on the outside wall and *under* the stairs, there's a handy little space just waiting to take a lavatory and wash basin at minimum expense. Meantime the drains are probably just outside, so with luck, it will merely be a matter of knocking one hole in the wall for the soil and waste pipe to join up with them and another hole to give you a tiny window or ventilation grid. But again, check that the idea is economically feasible (the drains may be round the back of the house, for instance) by getting a few plumbers' estimates. And whatever plumbing improvements you're contemplating, make sure you've got Planning Permission (only needed if you're going to knock a new window in the wall), and Building Permission (utterly essential, and only given after so many 'ifs' and 'buts' that you'll get to know the Building Inspector better than your milkman). For more about the specialist officers who are concerned in such building work, *3.1.

Making a gallery

Sometimes a room has a lot of space—unusable space between you and the ceiling that just gets ignored. But is it unusable? If you've bought a flat in an old house and the rooms are about 12 ft high, consider slipping in a gallery with a ladder or staircase leading up to it. In a living room, this can make a 'separate' dining room—even an open plan kitchen-cum-dining-room if you're prepared to spend extra for the plumbing. What it can't make, however, is a bedroom, because the fire regulations veto any situation where you have to go through a 'day room' to escape, should fire break out in the night. The only exception is if you live in a bedsitter flat, where you're already sleeping in a day room. Then you can make yourself a gallery bedroom—though you'll have to remember to make the bed so it always looks neat and attractive.

Although the open gallery must look light and airy from down below, it's got to be solidly constructed. Here you'll need an architect or building surveyor to calculate the load, and see you through all the rules and regulations so you get Building Permission (Planning Permission won't be needed because the gallery won't show externally). However good it looks, a rickety structure won't do. You'll probably need a steel beam running from wall to wall and/or some pillars for support. Also deep floor joists, and an efficient rail for safety. If you choose a conventional staircase, it will be beset with regulations about depths of tread and steepness, but it's certainly the easiest to get up and down and can look unobtrusive butted up against the wall. Spiral staircases look terrific (these have to pass the Building Inspector too), but they're easy to slip down if you're in a hurry. A ladder doesn't have to comply with any regulations (it's classed as a movable structure), but it's only for the young, energetic and preferably teetotal.

Converting the cellar or basement

Cellars were never meant to be lived in. Before the days of damp-proof courses, they *were* the damp-proof courses because they absorbed all the moisture before it reached the actual living areas. Even if there were windows they weren't meant to provide adequate ventilation but were an afterthought to help you distinguish the Château Neuf from the Nuits St Georges. This means that the moment you try to convert a cellar into a habitable room (and it can make a perfect kids' playroom or open plan kitchen and dining room), all the powers that be are going to be breathing down your neck to make sure you comply with today's improved living standards.

With an ambitious project like this, it's essential to employ an architect or building surveyor from the outset. He'll steer you through the problems of getting Planning Permission (needed, because you'll be changing the cellar's use from storage to living accommodation, and altering the external appearance of the house by making or enlarging the window). And he'll steer you through the even more complicated problems of getting Building Permission. These are legion. 'Habitable underground rooms', as they're known by local authorities, must have an internal height of 7 ft 6 in. This means that if your cellar's only 6 ft high, you've got to excavate downwards. Of course any small local builder's team can burrow away in the ground for you quite cheaply. But it takes an expert to organise a test dig and make sure the extra depth isn't going to extend below the foundations dangerously, undermining the entire structure of the house; also to make sure that any drainage runs survive the spades and pickaxes and comply with modern requirements.

Next you're going to need efficient damp-proof coursing, not just in the new floor you're building, but in the existing walls as well. This won't be cheap, but it's one of the first things a Building Inspector or District Surveyor will look for when he makes his inspection rounds.

Rules about light and air

Finally (and this is where many promising cellars have to give up all hopes of being converted), you need adequate lighting and ventilation. There are rigid rules about the size of window required for an underground room (underground being any room where the floor level is 3 ft below that of the street outside). First, your window or windows must be equal to at least $\frac{1}{10}$ of the room's floor area, and 50 per cent of them must be openable to provide the required ventilation. (You'll also need to provide 'permanent' ventilation; either an air-brick in the wall, or one of those hideous-looking spinning discs in the window.) Next, you have to have an unobstructed view (bushes and trees don't count) for at least 10 ft from your window. Fortunately this rule isn't as restrictive as it sounds, because the 10 ft is measured at an angle of 30°; in other words, you could have a pavement 6 ft away from your window, and provided no one had erected a bus shelter on it, you *might* manage to pass muster.

We say might, because here the plot thickens. Unless you have 2 ft of unrestricted space either side of the window, it will only count as $\frac{1}{7}$ of the floor space, even if it actually measures $\frac{1}{10}$. This means the wall dividing your front basement area from your neighbour's, or even your own front door steps, could foul up your well-laid plans.

Converting a loft or attic

This is another ambitious project that's ideal for a kids' playroom or an extra bedroom or two. But again, it's sensible to employ an architect or building surveyor from the outset, or hire a firm of loft conversion specialists who'll take the entire job off your hands, from getting permission from the local authority to doing the actual building work. This is because loft conversions are not always economically feasible—and you might as well find out before you spend too much money. The chances are you won't need Planning Permission (this depends on whether or not you put in a new

window), but you'll certainly need Building Permission, and this is where the snags may arise.

The first thing to check is the fire regulations. If conversion turns a two-storey house into a three-storey one, theoretically the rule book demands that you isolate *all* internal stairways, adjoining halls and landings within a fire-resistant structure, and make all doors leading off into habitable rooms fire-resistant too. This is a horribly costly procedure—so costly in fact, that unless you can get a 'waiver' (legal permission absolving you from complying with certain requirements) relaxing the regulations and saying you only have to isolate your *new* stretch of staircase, you're probably better off forgetting the whole enterprise.

Next you should check your roof construction. If your house has been

Left and below: This once-gloomy cellar was a maze of small rooms and cubby holes before it got knocked into one all-purpose sitting, eating, working and playing area, with the addition of some steel beams to hold the ground floor up. Huge work table in the kitchen area incorporates a stainless steel sink with waste disposal unit at the far end; marble pastry slab and electric ring for sauce-making at the near end. Living area leaves plenty of room for the kids to charge about in. PS. The plastering bill was nil everywhere but on the ceiling, because the owners preferred the original bare bricks—and luckily they were in good enough condition to stand exposure.

Graham Henderson

built fairly recently it will probably be constructed with trussed rafters and as it's impossible to remove a single one of these without weakening all the others, you'll find yourself getting involved with major roof reconstruction. This is even more prohibitively expensive than complying with fire regulations, so again, you could well find yourself having to abandon the idea.

The third thing to check is that your loft will measure 7 ft 6 in. high internally, over at least half its floor area, once it's converted (that's 8 ft 2 in. unconverted, because new floor joists and floor will take up 8 in. of space). If you haven't got enough floor area with the right height, your loft won't get approved as 'habitable'—though an easy solution could be to construct a dormer window, which projects from the sloping roof and provides more headroom.

These are just the major stumbling blocks. You're going to have to provide deeper floor joists (the existing ones will only have been meant to hold up empty space) and you'll need to provide a staircase. As mentioned earlier, fixed staircases are beset with enough building regulations to fill the rest of this chapter. Even so, retractable ladders aren't such a good idea. They're usually very steep, they rarely have a handrail on both sides, and if they're made of aluminium, they make a hideous clatter as you walk up and down them. Something worth remembering if there are bedrooms on the floor below.

Adding on an extension

A ground floor extension provides the perfect solution if an elderly relation comes to live with you. There'll be no stairs to climb and it'll feel like a private wing—especially if you can afford to lay on a water supply, so he or she can wash and make a cup of tea in peace.

The Sunday papers are full of advertisements for 'home extensions' that are merely sun lounges. They come in self-assembly panels for you or the supplier to erect and all Planning and Building Permissions are obtained for you in the cheap package-deal price. Great—except they're usually a mass of glass and timber that's freezing in winter, and to make them habitable— something that involves double glazing the windows, cladding the walls to comply with fire and insulation regulations, insisting on a solid roof with an internal height of 7 ft 6 in. etc.—you could end up spending as much as if you'd gone for a custom-built construction in the first place.

You don't need Planning Permission (but *3.2) for an extension at the back of your house, provided it doesn't enlarge your original house by more than 1,750 cu ft or $\frac{1}{10}$, whichever is the greater, and subject to a maximum of 4,000 cu ft. But you will need it for an extension to the front or side of your home. This is because it shows from the road and the local authority may insist you build your extension from the same materials as your house—no easy matter if it's an old flintstone building, or made from bricks that are no longer manufactured today (*3.3).

Incidentally, think twice about putting an extension on the side if you're going to seal off the rear of your property; you could find yourself having to carry fuel and dustbins through the house. One possible solution is to build a first-floor extension up on pillars, making a carport below. And don't presume it's possible to add a spare room above your garage. Quite probably, neither the foundations nor the garage walls were intended to take any extra weight, and you'll find yourself having to start completely from scratch.

Building regulations are extremely complicated and you will need an architect or building surveyor to sort them out for you. He'll deal with the problem of *drains:* complications arise when you want to build your extension over existing ones.

Boundaries: You'll have to get permission from your neighbour to build right up to one, as your foundations are going to be constructed under his land.

Foundations: They need to be on firm ground to avoid subsidence, not ground that was made up from its natural level at some previous time.

Fire regulations: All inside walls need to be fire-resistant. So do outside walls when they come within 3 ft of a boundary, and you may find restrictions placed on the number of 'unprotected' doors and windows you're allowed.

Insulation: Thermal insulation is specified, according to types of construction.

Sufficient light: If your extension's added on to a window wall instead of a solid wall, it must not obstruct the light from that window unless the room inside has another window that meets with building regulation requirements. Otherwise, the answer can be to remove the window wall and extend the whole room—provided, of course, there's enough space outside the new window to serve the enlarged room.

Adequate ventilation: Again, your extension musn't interfere with the ventilation in an existing room.

Efficient damp-proof coursing: This must be provided in the floor and in the walls.

These are just a few of the points an expert will be taking care of for you. And like all of the conversions mentioned above, they don't begin to tackle areas like wiring your new living space for electricity, or putting in plumbing if it's to be used for a kitchen or bathroom (like halls, these are classed as 'non-habitable' rooms, which relaxes a few regulations); or extending your central heating system, or laying the floors (solid concrete floors are best if you want to lay tiles, suspended wood floors if you want to fit carpets) or plastering the walls. Extending your home won't be an easy job. You'll need nerves of steel but when it's all over, you'll be able to sit back and feel justifiably proud of yourself.

Note This chapter is only intended for guidance. Everything in it is true in general but there are of course exceptions and it is impossible here to cover every situation. It's meant to give you a *rough* idea of what you're in for—not replace the expert advice you're going to need. You will find details of some helpful organisations and publications in the *Notes* to this chapter.

4 CONVERTING A WHOLE HOUSE

If you need nerves of steel for an extension, you'd be better off not having any at all for a thorough conversion. It's easy to fall for a neglected two-up-and-two-down and start visualising it with a lick of paint, a sparkling new front door and pretty roller blinds at the windows, but between the reality and the dream come months of dust, rubble and worry.

There are also, as always, money problems. Can you afford to buy the house outright? Building societies are hardly likely to lend on down-at-heel properties, so you may have to. Can you afford to pay for the building works? Even if you get a Discretionary Grant, of which more below, it often comes through when the house is finished (*4.1) whereas the builder wants paying as the work proceeds. Can you afford to live somewhere else while the work is going on? Apart from the fact that builders won't like

Small Edwardian house after conversion, standing out from its neighbours like a shirt in a detergent commercial, with its proud owners just about to take the baby for a walk. Note the dormer window in the roof, needed to give enough light and head-room to the loft conversion.

Graham Henderson

The master bedroom on the ground floor, along with the nursery that opens directly onto the back garden. Atmosphere is sympathetically but not slavishly Edwardian, with the original fireplace cherished instead of ripped out, and junk-shop buys playing up the nostalgic mood. Note how the modern louvred-pine wardrobes stop at the picture rail so the proportions of the room remain intact.

having you under their feet, you *can't* live there when there's no domestic supply of electricity or water. Unless you can get over this big financial hump, the really neglected bargains—and these are the ones that attract the biggest Discretionary Grants—go to the property developers, who promptly divide them into flats and sell them for more individually than the original houses cost.

But presuming you've managed to get a mortgage (and local authorities often look more kindly on old properties than building societies, especially if they come in one of their environmental areas), find yourself an architect, architectural consultant (*4.2) or building surveyor right away. Don't go it alone unless you're determined to have a nervous breakdown. It's not just a matter of interpreting rules and regulations but a matter of being able to handle human beings, who'll take you for a ride if they sense any weakness.

How to find an architect or building surveyor

Not many people like 'cut-and-carve' jobs, as they're known in the trade. It's fiddly work, it's much more difficult than building a new house, and it's never going to win anyone a prestigious design award. The best way of finding an architect is by personal recommendation (the worst way, incidentally, is to use an architect friend; don't, if you value the friendship!). Failing that, you could ask your local authority architect, who'll know who's doing most of the conversions in your area. If you still draw a blank, you can write to or telephone (01-580-5533) the Clients' Advisory Service at the Royal Institute of British Architects (RIBA), at 66 Portland Place, London W1. It won't be allowed to recommend anyone, but it will send you a list of suitable names, or put you in touch with your nearest Allied Society, who'll do the same. Alternatively, you can look up the RIBA *Directory of Practices* direct (it should be in any big reference library). This shows which architects are interested in small-scale jobs like conversions—though you may find they won't be bothered with anything where the building works come to less than £2,500.

Either way, once you've compiled your list don't stick a pin in it and hope for the best. Contact all the possibles and ask to see some examples of their conversion work. If at all possible, go and look at them—then you can ask the owner for a blow-by-blow account which will be far more revealing than looking at a glossy set of photographs. Be wary of taking on a young, inexperienced architect who needs the work. He may be a budding Christopher Wren—but practical, working knowledge is more important than artistic talent for cutting and carving.

Minimum RIBA fees are 13 per cent of the cost of conversion works for jobs up to £2,500 and 12½ per cent for jobs between £2,500 and £8,000 (we'll tell you what you get for your money shortly). It is possible to ask for a 'partial service' that only comes to about 3 per cent of the cost of the conversion works. Here the architect prepares working sketches, but leaves you to the tender mercies of the builder, a situation in which you could spend more on mistakes than you save on his fees.

The best way of finding a building surveyor who does conversions is, again, by personal recommendation. If this isn't forthcoming, try your local authority architect, or write for a likely list to the Royal Institution of Chartered Surveyors, 12 Great George Street, London SW1. His fees will probably be based on the RIBA scale—and again, ask to see some of his conversions before you commit yourself.

What he does for your money

The simplest way of explaining what an architect, architectural consultant or building surveyor will do for you (some do more than others—how much and how many site visits they're prepared to make is something you must establish *before* employing them) is to give a typical conversion schedule. This one assumes you're applying for a Discretionary Grant and using an architect; if not, mentally amend references as you read through.

Help with the preliminaries: Your architect will help you fill up your Discretionary Grant application form, and if you own the property freehold, an additional form giving the local authority permission to inspect the Land Registry records. He'll also make sure you get any building society's approval, and the freeholder's if you own only a lease. Should there be any doubt about whether you're eligible for a grant, he'll visit the local authority and get it agreed in principle—no use wasting time on something that isn't going to happen.

This is when he'll discuss the proposed conversion with you in general terms. You must know roughly what you want: how many rooms, whether you want to sleep upstairs or downstairs, whether you want to retain the house's character or re-vamp it completely.

Pointing out the possibilities: He'll measure the house and draw up precise plans of it as it stands. He'll have a good idea of what's

This ground floor bathroom was left over from the days when the house was full of bed-sitters. All it needed was new sanitary ware, some spanking white wall tiling, and natural cork tiles on the floor. But there's no modernising for modernisation's sake. The original door stays, panels attractively accentuated with wallpaper—much more sympathetic than a new, faceless flush door would have been.

Graham Henderson

possible—whether the local authority will allow a back extension, whether you'll be allowed to raise the roof and build another storey, whether you'll have to leave the front of the house exactly as it is to match the others in the road.

On the basis of his know-how, and within the limitations imposed, at this stage you have to decide *exactly* what you want, right down to positions of light fittings and central heating radiators. It isn't easy when the house is bleak and anonymous but now's the time to decide you want recessed lights in the ceiling that's going to be lowered, or ducted warm air heating under the floorboards that have got to come up anyway. Once the final plans are drawn up, your architect will charge for every alteration he has to make to them—and of course, once building work begins, even small changes are likely to cost big money.

Detailed specifications: He'll draw up detailed plans of the scheme you've agreed between you. He'll also write a specification of works, setting out clearly what the various tradesmen will need to do. *Note:* Even if you're trying to do the conversion yourself, at least employ an architect for this specialised task. It may seem straightforward to write 'Excavate floor one foot in depth', but unless you add 'and remove excavated earth', you'll get left with a mound or charged extra to take it away. Builders take everything literally and you have to spell it out for them.)

Obtaining permission: He'll send plans and specification of works to the local authority for approval. This could take two to three months to come through. Once Planning Permission is given it's final; Building Permission is subject to inspection and approval by the Building Inspector at various stages of the work. Meantime, your architect will send plans and specification of works out to at least three builders for tender (i.e. for them to quote on). He'll also answer any of their queries.

Choosing from the tenders: Within a month or so the tenders will start coming in, and he'll go through them with you. If all the estimates are similar, he may well recommend the cheapest, but if one is much cheaper than the others, he'll probably try and steer you clear of it. This isn't because he's trying to push up his percentage. It's because builders go broke at the drop of a hat (they annually top the list of firms that go bankrupt) and if you accept an unrealistic estimate, it's your job they'll go broke on. Once this happens, you're in trouble. No builders like 'pick-up' jobs, and they always put in very high prices for finishing off someone else's work. Even so, should this happen, your architect will rightly advise you against turning yourself into a 'builder' and employing direct labour—a nightmare situation where you'd probably find yourself getting conned right, left and centre.

Breaking down the estimate: If you're applying for a Discretionary Grant, he'll ask the chosen builder to supply a broken-down estimate for submission to the local authority. As this needs to be very detailed (the builder will have to quote for everything, from £400 for electrical wiring to £5 for repairing a door), it could take at least another fortnight.

Applying for the grant: As soon as he receives local authority approval, your architect will submit the completed grant application form and so on, referred to previously, along with plans, specification of works and broken-down builder's estimate, to whoever is dealing with grants at the local authority. This is where things come to a grinding halt. Getting Discretionary Grant approval usually takes at least two months; if you get impatient and start building in the meantime, *you forfeit any chance of a grant altogether*. (Your architect may speed things up by applying for the grant as soon as the builder's broken-down estimate comes in, but only if he's sure his scheme's going to get local authority approval. If it doesn't, he'll only have to scrap his original grant application, and waste time and money starting from scratch with the amended scheme.)

Setting out the liabilities: As soon as the grant approval arrives, he'll draw up a formal RIBA contract between you and the builder, to determine each side's liabilities, set out methods of payment, make sure the building and the people working on it are insured, and so on.

Let him give the orders: He'll instruct the builder to start work, and if you want to avoid costly mistakes, make it clear you're 'only the owner'. All instructions must come from your architect. Never mind if an appealing young workman says 'Is it all right if I do such-and-such?' Even if it looks a harmless amendment, he's only interested in making his life easier—and there's bound to be a reason why it has to be difficult.

Pay as you go: As regards money, the builder will probably want to be paid on fortnightly or monthly certificates. This is where your architect is vital. At each certificate-time (presuming you stipulated this when you gave him instructions) he'll come and check that the work is satisfactory, answer any queries, and make sure you never sign a cheque for more work than has been done. The builder will probably complain bitterly about this last part, but harden your heart: the best guarantee anyone ever has of getting a conversion properly finished is that the builder's done more work than he's been paid for!

Your architect will also keep an eye on 'extras' and see they don't spiral out of all proportion. These always arise somewhere along the line with old buildings, and you should keep a reserve sum of money to cover them.

Putting things right: When the work is completed, he'll make a final inspection and compile a schedule of defects for the builder to make good. Once these have been carried out, the final account will be agreed and 95 per cent of the contract sum will be released to the builder. *Note:* Of course, if you've been so generous with your certificates that the builder's already had 100 per cent, the chances are he'll vanish and leave you in the lurch.)

The local authority will make their inspection too, and if the work meets the required standard (something your architect will have ensured), they pay over the grant money.

A last look around: Six months later, when you've lived in the house long enough to discover defects that missed the previous inspection, or have developed since then—central heating is notorious for playing up after a month or two—your architect will carry out a further inspection. Once the builder makes these defects good, your architect will release the final 5 per cent of the contract sum to him. He'll also have finished working for you, so after all the money and headaches he's saved you, please don't make him wait for his professional fees!

PS on conversions

When undertaking a conversion, get your priorities right. Don't spend so long dithering with details that you hold up the basic building works and cost yourself a small fortune. Make up your mind early about what tiles you want on the kitchen floor, what sanitary ware you want in the bathroom, what knobs you want on the doors and so on. And don't expect the builder to be able to act on your decision immediately; the ceramic tiles you fancy may have a 16-week delivery date.

Finally, don't spend a lot of money on wall coverings. New plaster takes

1

2

Graham Henderson

36

Facing page 1 and 2: Two views of the living/dining room that runs the length of the first floor, along with a large landing and tiny second bathroom. (Of course, the owners *could* have lived on the ground floor in the conventional way—but that would have wasted the best view of the park.) Gothic window, with landing behind it, came from a church near Aylesbury; was inserted without too much difficulty because the wall wasn't load-bearing. Beautiful pine floor had to be newly-laid—even though there was an equally beautiful pine floor there previously. This is because once the owners announced their plans to convert the loft up above, which would make the house a three-storey dwelling, the Fire Regulations demanded a special fire-resistant floor. Originally, the first floor consisted of several small rooms. Getting the unwanted walls knocked down was easy, but as some of them were load-bearing, a massive steel beam (clad in pine and clearly visible), had to be inserted to keep the ceiling up. Open pine staircase leads up to the loft.

3 Loft conversion was well worth the expense, because it provided this fabulous guest bedroom, and an equally fabulous study at the back of the house.

months to dry out so however much you want to impress friends with your new home, it's lunacy to hang an expensive grasspaper that'll go mouldy with damp. Much better to ask for an all-white-emulsion builder's finish. Then the walls will have time to dry out, you'll get a chance to fill the settlement cracks and you'll have time to make friends with your new surroundings and choose the decorations at leisure.

QUALIFYING FOR A LOCAL AUTHORITY GRANT

The Standard Grant has been around for a long time. You can demand it from your local authority by right if your house, which must be freehold or have at least a five-year lease to run, lacks any of the following: A bath or shower (maximum amount allowable £30); a wash basin (£10); an inside lavatory (£50); a kitchen skink (£15); a full hot and cold water supply to the bath or shower (£45), the wash basin (£20) and the kitchen sink (£30). This gives a ceiling figure of £200 in normal circumstances, but if you have to pipe in a supply of water for the first time, build a septic tank because there's no main drainage, or build an extension because there's nowhere in the house to fit a bathroom, the sum goes up to a maximum of £450.

Of course, it doesn't come as a straight gift with Green Shield stamps. For every £1 the local authority gives you, you have to provide £1 out of your own pocket (in other words, you have to pay half). This means that if a plumber puts in a quote of £200 for installing sanitary ware, you'll only get £100, not the £200 maximum; if a builder puts in a quote of £650 for erecting a bathroom extension, you'll only get £325, not the £450 maximum. What's more, the works that qualify for a grant will have to be approved by the local authority before they'll pay over the money. They're interested in raising the standard of houses—so they want to see a professional job, not a do-it-yourself enthusiast's botch-up. (Incidentally, and this should nip DIY aspirations in the bud, do remember you won't get any allowance for supplying your own labour—only for the cost of the raw materials you use.

Also that you have to complete the work within a year.)

The Discretionary Grant

These amounts of money aren't to be sniffed at, but if you can possibly manage it (and this is where building societies are likely to prove a stumbling block) buy a house that's so old it needs substantial modernisation. This way it will be eligible for a Discretionary Grant and here the maximum is £1,000. Again, you have to find £1 for every £1 the local authority provides; you have to own the freehold or a lease that has five years to run; and the finished work has to gain local authority approval; in this case, there's a 12-point standard it has to meet (*4.3).

The bumper sum is attractive enough on its own—but Discretionary Grants have another advantage over Standard Grants: up to half of the amount allowed can go towards structural repairs. The important thing to realise is that there's no Discretionary Grant for repairs alone. Buy an old house with faulty electrical wiring, sanitary ware pitted with smallpox, an ancient geyser that wheezes every time it produces hot water and a damp-proof course that's letting through the damp—and quite possibly you won't be eligible for a penny. But buy a house that never had a bathroom in the first place, and where a damp-proof course was never inserted, and not only will providing them count as modernisation—but you'll be allowed an equal amount for essential repairs, such as getting the electricity re-wired and replacing the ancient geyser with a more efficient form of water heating.

No strings attached: The lovely thing about the Discretionary Grant (and the Standard Grant, come to that) is that there are no strings attached. At present there's nothing to stop you (apart from your social conscience) buying a tumbledown cottage, getting the maximum grant, selling it at a profit and moving on to do it all over again. Even though Discretionary Grants are given at the local authority's discretion, many are unlikely in practice to turn down an application unless they know it's coming from a property developer.

Playing 'Monopoly': Which brings us to the last phase of the Discretionary Grant. Although the maximum is £1,000 for converting a house into one home, if the house has three or more storeys, you can get up to £1,200 for each self-contained flat you make out of it. This means in theory that if you convert it into three flats, you should be able to sell off one, to cover the cost of the house; sell off another, to cover the conversion costs and with luck, leave yourself with about £3,000's worth of grant to play with; and live in the third flat completely free (but *4.4). Or sell it off and start all over again, until you eventually end up with a whole house for free. Whether you make lots of money or lose the little you've got (and you only hear of the successes, not the many failures), could depend almost entirely on your architect, architectural consultant or building surveyor. Fortunately his fees are eligible for a grant too, so whether you're simply adding a bathroom, converting a house, or dividing it into flats, subject to the maximum amounts allowable, you'll be getting his services at half the price.

5 HOW TO LIVE WITH THE COLOURS YOU LIKE

Everyone has a favourite colour. You may find it in the friendly warm colours—the yellows, oranges, pinks and reds; or the sophisticated cool colours such as the blues, greens, purples and whites (*5.1). But whatever your choice, picking the basic colour is the easy part of decorating a room. What's difficult is knowing how to use it, because left on its own, it merely survives; surrounded by conflicting colours, it withers and dies. In fact to make it live, you have to enhance it by building up an interplay of colour relationships. This means that, right from the start, you need to know the general effect you are after. (And if you're not sure, paint the walls white and wait; soak up the feel of your surroundings till you know what's needed.) A room can be satisfying only as a totality, so don't let yourself be swayed into concentrating on individual features.

As a simple guide, take one of three basic approaches. Pick one colour and stick to it, varying the shades to relieve monotony. Use neutral 'non-colours' instead, dropping in a bright accent colour for interest. Or if you're very sure of yourself, contrast strong colours.

However you go about it, make sure that your most expensive item, the carpet, is in the colour that is to remain a constant. Also, bear in mind that, although you may be decorating only one room, sooner or later you'll be decorating the adjoining room and the room adjoining that. Aim to make one room flow into the other, perhaps by carrying through the main or accent colour of one room as the contrast colour of the next. This way a continuity of mood can be created, turning a series of unrelated parts into a relaxing whole.

Pick one colour and stick to it
One colour, used with care and a splash of imagination, can decorate a complete room single-handed. The secret is to choose a key pattern first, either in your carpet, fabric or wallpaper: a pattern that incorporates several tones of the colour you've decided on. From then on you just make use of the designer's advice for free, and transplant the individual colour tones used in his pattern on to your walls, floor and furniture.

Forget the old wives' tale about clashing colours; it may come as a shock

Sale Stone & Senior settings Diana Austen

Sale Stone & Senior settings Diana Austen

Sale, Stone & Senior; setting, Diana Austen

Sale, Stone & Senior; setting, Diana Austen

Previous pages, above, left: Proof that blue isn't necessarily a cold, wintry colour—an intimate bedroom that wouldn't have anyone shivering between the sheets. Because it keeps to deep shades of blue that could get heavy, the bedspread and dramatic drapes are patterned in white. Walls are papered in a rich midnight blue and two perspex lampshades throw pools of subdued light over the cornflower-blue military chests. This plays up the warmth of the brassbound corners, the bright red clock and the red and purple anemones.

Below, left: Deep greens are so restful they can send you to sleep. Living room over-the-page makes sure you won't nod off before the Epilogue by introducing acid-sharp lemon and lime in the floor-length window blind. Because the blind's crisp and astringent, you *could* play safe and use deep, passive greens without the result looking dull. But here, caution's been thrown to the winds. A brilliant wet-grass green carpets the floor, covers the walls in a slightly darker shade, and upholsters the armchairs too. Deep-green leafy plants soften the effect, and the white pendant fitting (an absolute essential), suffuses the whole setting in a gentle light.

Above, right: Sunny but not sweltering dining room takes its colour cue from the formally-sprigged print of the floor-length window blind. The golden yellow is repeated in the plain, textured wallpaper and the seat cushions; the mustard in the close-pile fitted carpet. And before the result can set solid as cold custard, the white is repeated in the window frame and skirting, and gives everything a crisp visual lift. White *Arkana* table, lit by a dandelion yellow pendant, provides a larger area of light relief, and picture frames, which could have been yellow, prefer to hint at the colour with mellow maple.

Below, right: Red on the rampage doesn't have to be hot and overpowering—not if you introduce plenty of white to help it keep its cool. Warm but not stifling living room on the previous page lowers the temperature with white sheers at the windows and white paint on the walls. Also with 'cool' modern furniture—the outlines are clean and sophisticated, instead of cosy and claustrophobic. General effect is friendly but restful— proof that red doesn't have to be action-packed as a fire-engine. On the floor, square-patterned carpet 'clashes' cherry, scarlet and maroon to prove they can co-exist peacefully.

to your eyes initially, but all shades of one colour will blend together. Turquoise will go with midnight blue, sharp lime with emerald, flame with fuschia red, bitter lemon with mustard. Your only problem will be balancing the different colour 'weights', but the key pattern can help you here too. Notice which tones have been used in which quantity and copy the proportions. Don't forget that every scheme needs neutral tones for light relief—so when in doubt, add white or off-white to the mixture.

Forget the clichés: Which colour you choose is up to you. Again, forget rigid clichés about blue being a cold colour and red being a hot one. Generally speaking they are of course, but a blue mixed with enough yellow to become turquoise looks warm and sunny; a red mixed with enough blue to become maroon looks cold and gloomy. In fact the only cliché that holds good (and please forget the one about dark colours 'lowering' a ceiling—all they do is make you think 'Ah-ha—they've tried to lower the ceiling') is that strong colours make a room seem smaller. So avoid the one colour approach unless your room is large, or you're prepared to say (and why not?) 'It's small and to hell with it'.

Restfulness can be boring; The advantage of one-colour rooms is that you can't go wrong. If you're ready to take the plunge with 100 per cent conviction, the results are bound to look 100 per cent professional. However, the disadvantage is that unless you're starting from scratch, or can take your lead from existing carpets and upholstery, you're going to have to make some expensive replacements. Easy enough to whizz around with a paintpot painting walls, shelves and doors—but there's not much you can do with a deep green carpet when you're after a bright yellow one.

The other disadvantage is rather more long term. Although one-colour rooms are especially restful—shades blend into each other without visual disruption—after a few years the very restfulness might have you climbing up the walls with boredom. In other words, don't plump for this approach unless you're sure you're still going to like being surrounded by your chosen colour in ten years time. Or keep it for rooms you don't spend much time in, like the dining room, or a hall that'll have visitors paying you compliments before they've even got over the threshold.

Choose cool non-colours

Using non-colours and dropping in small splashes of accent colour is even more foolproof. It's much more flexible too, because once you've got your neutral shell, you can keep it indefinitely and change your 'colour scheme' with the minimum expense and effort.

Getting the basic shell is easy; whites, creams, beiges and oatmeals haven't the strength to fight, so however you combine them, you're on sure ground. The only snag, if you can call it a snag, is that you've got to pick good quality items. When you're relying on subtlety for interest, every detail has to be able to survive close scrutiny. There'll be no colour or pattern to distract attention from second-best, so don't invite people to look again and again unless what they're going to see improves with acquaintance.

Taking the rough with the smooth: This is why texture plays such an important part in non-colour rooms. It provides warmth and interest, and without it, the result would look smooth, faceless and anonymous. Which doesn't mean that you *have* to strip your walls back to the bricks and paint them white, buy a rugged long-pile carpet, upholster your furniture in nubbly tweed, or hang coarse hessian at the windows. The changes in texture can be much less aggressive, and in a non-colour context, even a 'smooth' beige Wilton carpet will begin to look rough against a shiny white leather settee. (Incidentally, though those examples are expensive, picking good quality items needn't be.) If you can't afford good carpet, for instance, natural rush matting or sanded-and-sealed floorboards plus a shaggy goatskin rug, make alternatives that are good in their own right. Either way, provided you mix the rough with the smooth, you'll find your room has plenty of character despite the lack of colour. And a bonus that could make you a non-colour convert for ever—because of the lack of colour, your room will look much larger than it really is.

Small dashes of colour: From now onwards, it's easy to add a colour scheme. The only thing to remember is that every splash of colour will zing out with twice its usual intensity, so keep the quantities small. This way you can use as many as you like; a neutral room with small dashes of all the

Previous pages, left: Impeccably-elegant Georgian living room takes 'non-colour' quite literally. Walls, ceiling, carpet, upholstery—even Roman blinds at the window and lamp on the coffee table—are in a pale shade of ecru. But the room's vibrant with colour all the same, thanks to the dazzling-patterned cushions, that sing out with twice their usual colour-intensity in the neutral setting. **Right:** Not quite so obviously non-colour bedroom (the honey-pine wardrobe wall and mellow oil paintings provide a basis of colour), has a neutral grey carpet, black, grey and white bedspread, and plain white walls and storage. Colour comes in small bright splashes—a vase of red, green and yellow paper flowers, a red and ferociously loud-looking alarm clock, a zingy red box, and a red vase, full of dried flowers to complement the natural pine tones.

four primary colours always looks a knock-out. Alternatively, there's no reason why you shouldn't stick at just one or two colours. A few plain cushions in pink and orange, a patterned pink and orange roller blind, and a vase of pink and/or orange flowers will bring your room alive with colour. And when you get tired of them, it only costs a few pounds to ring the changes completely with plain blue and green cushion covers, a patterned blue and green roller blind and a vase of blue flowers or some green leafy plants.

Contrasting strong colours

Putting one strong colour against another is the most ambitious approach of all—and the most popular with beginners, who rush in where even the experts (*5.2) tread with caution. We'd like to be able to rattle off a list of can't-go-wrong rules, but alas, there's no foolproof formula for success unless you steal one (and we'll tell you how to in a minute). The sad fact is that you've either got an instinctive 'eye' and can anticipate how one colour is going to react when you put it against another, or you haven't, and you could get involved in expensive mistakes.

The trouble is that colour develops a life of its own as soon as you put it next to another colour. Paint one wall a bright pink and you'll know exactly where you are. But paint the wall next to it a brighter orange and the pink beside it will fizzle into virtual extinction. Unless you can get the balance of strength just right (and this is something it's impossible to tell from the miserable square inches provided on paint cards), your colours are going to kill instead of complementing each other. And of course, the more colours you introduce, the bigger the element of risk—which is why it's best to confine yourself to just one, or at most, two contrasts.

Advice by the yard: If all that sounds downright discouraging, cheer up, because you can buy expert advice in any fabric department. All you need to do is choose a pattern you really like and feel you can live with. (Not that you have to live with it of course—just half a yard will usually be enough for you to make use of.) Then sit down and analyse it. There'll be years of experience in how the designer has contrasted one colour with another and what proportions he's decided to do it in. Work these out, transfer them to your own furnishings, and you should be assured of a successful result.

Even with this free design advice, play safe and avoid any contrast between expensive items like carpets (*5.3) and upholstery. Keep these the same colour, and then if you do make a mistake elsewhere, it will only take another pot of paint or some more rolls of wallpaper to put matters right. What's more, you'll be able to change the entire aspect of your room by choosing another contrast any time you start getting bored with your first one.

And talking of getting bored: the contrast approach to colour makes a natural follow-up to both one-colour and non-colour approaches. If you've grown thoroughly sick of an all-green room, for instance, simply keep the green carpet and armchairs, and introduce a different colour like red for the walls and curtains. And if you've had enough of cool, cool neutrals, hot them up with big expanses of colour where it doesn't cost much money to make the change.

Following pages, left: A non-colour scheme that turns into a contrast scheme. The neutral living room plays safe with a grey carpet and settee upholstered in flecky grey tweed—so they can stay constant while you ring the changes around them. Subtle shades-of-grey basics need careful handling—too dense a colour on the walls would drain them; pale pastels would look merely wishy-washy. On the left, a strong but not dominant sandstone provides the solution, and adds warmth and friendliness.

When you've got bored with it, switch to a patterned contrast—but make sure there's a colour link with the carpet and settee that form your starting point. On the right, swirly wallpaper has enough grey, black and white for continuity; enough tan and scarlet for contrast. Accessories make the impact stronger, but don't overdo them. A single scarlet cushion and a maple-framed picture are all that's needed for extra colour-emphasis.

Right: A one-colour scheme that turns into a contrast scheme. On the left, shaggy-pile moss-green carpet gives the cue for a plain Granny Smith green wallpaper and some shades-of-green cushions. White provides light relief, dazzling bright in the hand-crocheted Victorian bedspread, the painted bed-head and side table, and the white plastic lampshade.

But the day you wake up tired of green-with-everything, go for a contrast with the wallpaper on the right. A riot of unrelated colours at first glance, but the green leaves link with the carpet, the white background with the bedspread. And all it takes is some pink/yellow cushions, and an orange lampshade, to pull the scheme into a coherent whole.

6 LOOKING AT WINDOWS

The trouble with windows is that, like doors, they often get treated as an afterthought. This doesn't matter too much if they're perfectly positioned and proportioned—but often they're not, and then they need some crafty disguising.

Broadening a narrow window: Despite the swing to roller blinds and Venetians, you can't beat good old-fashioned curtains for softening the shape of awkward windows. Say you've got a tall, narrow window (about 2 ft wide, for instance), that's nearly as meagre as a gun-slit. Fake a window of much more generous proportions by fixing a 4 ft-wide curtain track or decorative pole above it and hanging luxurious floor-length curtains so they reveal all the window but just hide the frames at the sides (see page 51). This kind of fraud works well if you've got two windows of different widths along the same wall. Simply give them the same size track or decorative poles and hang the curtains to the sides identically—something that will be determined by the width of the narrower window. Then you'll have a look of perfect symmetry that'll fool everyone but the people passing by.

Disguising uneven sills: What if the two windows have different depths? If you live in a town and the view isn't worth looking at, soften the outline of the window sills with floor-length nets or sheers (see below) that stay drawn all the time. By day they'll diffuse the light softly, and by night you simply draw the main curtains over them. If you like the view or can't afford to lose any light, try faking equal depths with two rows of café curtaining—keeping the bottom row drawn to hide the window sills, and leaving the top row drawn back to let the light in. A double or treble row is a good idea if you have central heating radiators bang underneath your windows. They look bad enough in winter, when you shouldn't really keep them covered, but at least in summer you can keep the bottom row of curtains drawn to hide the ugly, metal hulk of them (see picture on page 52).

Bays and French windows: What can you do with those 1930s favourites, the bay window and the French window? Now that many curtain tracks bend quite happily round curves and corners, it's quite possible to curtain a bay in one clean sweep if you want to. The only snag is that during the day the bay looks very cold and naked, so it's often better to make several narrow curtains,

1 Narrow window looks much wider if you extend curtain track or decorative pole, and hang curtains so they just hide the window frame. This way, the eye thinks there's much more window either side. **2** Tricky but worthwhile treatment for a Georgian arch that would be spoiled by a straight heading. Curve plastic curtain track to fit arch, or simply screw eyelets direct into it. Make up curtain fabric to shape, remembering you'll need to cut for a wider arch to allow for pleating, and use a tape like RUFFLETTE'S *Autopleat.* Hook into permanent position (obviously the track itself won't be operational), and loop curtains back at sides during the day. Then to 'draw' the curtains at night, all you have to do is unloop them, and they fall together.

grouped in pairs at each window upright. Or fit individual roller blinds with decorative trims to each window and pull the main curtains over at night. As for the familiar T-shaped French window, its hard, ugly lines need plenty of pretty fabric to make it appealing. The most attractive solution (see picture on page 53), is to make floor length cover-all curtains that stay drawn back by day, and break up the harsh T-shape by adding matching café curtains that stay in place permanently.

Seeing out but not in

A room with a view works both ways, which is why many people keep net curtains drawn all day. Terylene nets have built-in whiteness that doesn't degenerate into grey; they're drip-dry too. Old-fashioned Nottingham lace needs more care but it's desperately pretty. (Wash *before* you make up the curtains to allow for shrinkage; thereafter, always damp-iron it and stretch the fabric back to shape as you go.) If the wind whips your curtains to the ceiling every time you open a window, sew an 'invisible' lead-shot-filled tape into the hems as you make them. About 10p a yard from most haberdashery departments. And if you live bang on a busy street, with no front garden to stop people peering in, buy a fabric called *Vero-sol*, about £2 a yard, 48 in. wide. From the inside it looks like a conventional net, but from the outside its one-sided aluminium coating renders it completely opaque.

See-through, yet 'solid': Sheers are big news in Scandinavia but are catching on slowly here. They're a kind of mid-point between nets and conventional fabrics, and because they're usually made of drip-dry *Dralon* or *Acrilan*, they're non-shrink and can be hung back at the windows soon after washing. See-through by day, they give privacy and diffuse incoming light softly, but by night they give the impression of 'solid' curtains. Use them on their own, with main curtains to draw over them, or for a really filmy, luxurious look, as main curtains over conventional net curtains. Or use them as a room divider that will create separate areas without making the room look smaller or darker. A good selection of nets and sheers is available from most large stores.

3 Two rows of café curtaining are ideal if people can peer into your home from the pavement. Then you can keep the upper row open to let in the light; the lower row closed against prying eyes. Make it three rows if you've got an ugly radiator under the window. Then you can keep the bottom row closed during the summer to hide it.

3

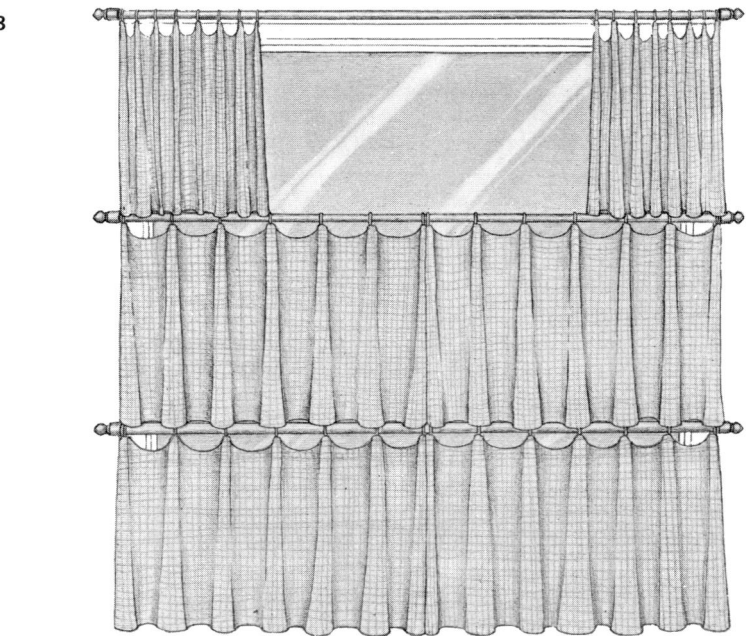

Buying curtain tracks

Apart from extra-strong brass rails for really weighty curtains, brass tracks have no advantage over plastic. Things to watch out for when you buy curtain tracks (*6.1): does the price include all the brackets, stops and gliders? do they come with cording sets?—something that saves wear and tear on curtains if they're so heavy you have to tug them back—can the track you're considering be bent to go round curves and corners? If you're hopeless at judging the number of hooks a curtain needs, but never find out till you're perched precariously on a table, buy something like *Swish De-Luxe* or *Faber 66* where you can hook the curtains to the rail in the comfort of your armchair, and then clip the rail to the brackets.

If you're not sure of your window measurements or may have to move house, buy extending track by firms like KIRSCH, HARRISON or WOOLWORTH. Or buy a GRABER spring tension rod that needs no fixing at all and simply expands to fit tightly into the window opening. If your home is in the process of being built or you're making a false ceiling, consider buying a recessed track (by a firm like SILENT GLISS); these are suitable for room dividers too.

Curtaining a Georgian arch: So far, no one makes a special track for those vast Georgian arches, so if you're lucky enough to have them and can't bear to spoil the shape with a straight heading, why not make non-drawing curtains

4 French windows make a harsh, ugly T-shape. Here, the lines are softened by café curtains that stay permanently drawn. Matching full-length curtains get drawn at night.

Roberta Edney

looped back at the sides to let the light in (see picture on page 51). This does mean cutting the curtain fabric to the shape of the arch, and either fixing a curved plastic curtain track (used in conjunction with special tape to give a high pleated heading that hides it) or screwing eyelets direct to the arch of the casement and hooking curtains (with standard curtain tape for ordinary gathers) into them.

Making curtains on a budget

In the days when curtain tracks were so hideous that everyone had to hide them behind pelmets, it was a waste of time using anything other than cheap, standard tape and hooks. After all, no one could *see* the curtain heading, and all that mattered was that the curtains should hang in even gathers. But now that pelmets (*6.2) are unnecessary *and* unfashionable, tracks need much more decorative headings and these can be quite an expensive item. You'll see what we mean if you compare the price of *Rufflette Standard* tape to *Rufflette Regis* tape for pencil pleats—the latter cost nearly five times as much. Not that the difference in cost ends there. When you're using standard tape for ordinary gathers, you need $1\frac{1}{2}$ times as much fabric as the width of the curtain track to get sufficiently generous-looking folds. But if you're using special tapes for pencil pleats, you need at least $2\frac{1}{4}$ times the width of the curtain track. Pinch pleats (*Rufflette Autopleat* tape costs nearly 7 times as much as *Standard* tape) can take even more, depending whether you go for single, double or treble pleats.

Economising without skimping: As nothing looks worse than skimped curtains, the best thing you can do is either use masses and masses of cheap fabric (ever thought of curtain lining on its own? it comes in a wide range of super colours), or use a little of a good fabric and simply let it hang flat. The latter works best with decorative poles (*6.3), and though these can cost a small fortune if they're made of solid wood or brass, you can buy very cheap plastic ones that look every bit as convincing. (Or alternatively, you can make your own with a broom handle or brass-cased tubing from an ironmonger, plus ordinary brass rings, though you'll have to buy proper brackets with adjustable screws so the pole doesn't slip as you draw the curtains.) Then pick a rich, heavy fabric that can stand on its own. Felt is ideal for this situation, because if you want scallops to compensate for the lack of folds, you can simply cut them out with a pair of scissors and not even bother with hemming.

All kinds of blinds

Of course, the cheapest way of economising on fabric is to make a roller blind. (As with all blinds, this presumes that your windows are attractively proportioned and don't need disguising). If you're 'rolling your own' (*6.4), go for a closely-woven cotton, sailcloth or PVC-coated fabric; anything heavier or finer will tend to bunch on the rollers. And if you're trying to fill a big picture window, make two or three small blinds rather than one big one, because seams down the middle will look unsightly and affect the way the blind hangs. If you're not much good at sewing but still want to use a particular fabric, perhaps because it matches the wallpaper you've used (this is a good way of integrating a tiny window into your scheme of things when it would look lost and silly in splendid isolation), there are several firms who'll make roller blinds to order (*6.5).

Ready-made roller blinds: Of course, most of the blind manufacturers make roller blinds in so many fade-proof colours and patterns, and with so many different decorative trims (*6.6), that you're quite likely to find what you want among their samples. They're ideal for tiny windows that would be swamped by curtains and especially for kitchens, where curtains near a cooker could easily go up in flames. Practical too, because some come in acrylic or vinyl-finished fabrics that can be wiped clean with a damp cloth; and even traditional cotton holland blinds have been 'beetled' (bumped with massive rollers until the fibres go flat and shiny-hard) so any dust sits on the surface and can simply be flicked off with a duster.

Venetian blinds: Whatever the manufacturers claim, Venetian blinds (*6.7) aren't so easy to clean. They're hell to dust, and even though the rust-free blinds unclip easily nowadays, it's still a major operation dunking them in the bathtub. Nevertheless, they're so neat and good-looking, it's small wonder they've spread from kitchens and bathrooms to all over the house. The main advantage is that they give you complete control over the amount of light you let in (the amount of heat too, if you're tired of being baked through your picture window every summer). The main disadvantage is that despite today's brilliant colour ranges, they still tend to look cold and clinical. One way round this is to use them with sheers or curtains for a softening effect. Another is to buy blinds with cedarwood slats—not cheap, but they add a lot of character, and they don't give a metallic clank when you close them.

Vertical blinds: These are rather like Venetian blinds, only the slats go up and down instead of horizontally (*6.8). They're ideal for picture windows, and especially for floor-to-ceiling patio windows or room dividers, because you can walk straight through them. The slats are much wider (usually about 4 in.), and thoroughly wipe-clean and practical, but as these blinds are expensive, and get cheaper in proportion as they get larger, they're only worth considering when you're thinking big.

Cheap but nice: Some of the best-looking blinds are some of the cheapest, so take heart. Paper pleated blinds (*6.9), concertina upwards at the pull of a cord, are much tougher than they sound, and survive quite sturdily provided you don't put them in a steamy kitchen or bathroom. So are reeded vinyl roll-up blinds (*6.10) which work on a cord and pulley system; however, if your window is tall, be prepared for a fairly bulky roll by the time they reach the top. Woven pine reed roll-up blinds *are* more expensive, but in natural pine or traditional dark green, they filter light in a Somerset Maughamish way that suggests tropical sunshine outside, whatever the weather. And that alone makes it worth looking at windows.

7 HANDLING PATTERN

Patterns should have 'handle with care' stamped all over them. They've got wills of their own, and unless you keep a very tight rein on them, they'll get completely out of control before you know what's hit you.

The simplest way to avoid getting punch-drunk is to buy one of the co-ordinated ranges where an expert's made sure in advance that everything will co-exist peacefully. It's the safest way too if you want to mix your patterns, something that takes a very sure eye for scale and proportion. The best-known example is probably SANDERSON's TRIAD range (*7.1). Here if you choose a boldly-patterned wallpaper, it will probably be teamed with: another patterned wallpaper, related in colour and design, but on a smaller, quieter scale; a plain wallpaper, picking out just one of the colours; a patterned fabric, related in colour and design to all three; a couple of plain fabrics, picking out the two main colours; and related plain and patterned roller blinds.

Linked from paper to pillowcases: MARY QUANT's ICI range, now out of production, was even more comprehensive. It's worth mentioning because it's the kind of thing that's done a lot in the u.s., and despite the fact that it proved ahead of its time here, it must be the shape of things to come. Although it only started off with one wallpaper (a gingham pattern available in four colours) that was enough to spark off: related wall friezes, paints, plain and patterned curtain fabrics and roller blinds, window nets, sheets, pillowcases, duvet covers, eiderdowns and even stretch covers to pull your upholstery into the scheme of things. In short, a complete can't-go-wrong kit and it's instructive to look at the pictures on pages 15 (above), 58 and 89, even though you can no longer buy the products.

The trouble with co-ordinated ranges is that they're not cheap; usually it's only 'up market' manufacturers (*7.2) who produce them. So if you can't afford them, or simply prefer to go-it-alone, here's a rough rule-of-thumb for how to go about it. The best way to restrain the exuberance of patterns is to keep them apart. Pick a patterned carpet (*7.3) or a patterned wallpaper or patterned curtains—never mix them together unless you're very confident—and even then keep your fingers crossed. Also make sure they're patterns you're going to be able to live with. As with colour, this is almost impossible to tell from a small sample, so try to see a large expanse of carpet before you commit

Sale, Stone & Senior; setting, Diana Austen

Secret of mixing patterns is to keep the scale and mood right—and everything else simple. Here, curtains at the window and tiles on the floor are of equal strength, so there's a balance of power instead of continual bickering. And as both patterns are neat and geometric, there's a sympathetic relationship from the word go. Everything else stays rigidly simple, with furniture positioned symmetrically to play up the geometric mood.

yourself; make the shop assistant unroll that bale of fabric; buy just one roll of wallpaper to begin with. Until you can see how the pattern repeats *en masse*, you've no way of knowing how big an impact it's going to make—and this doesn't just apply to scale. Even a small, innocuous design can give off a virulent Op-art dazzle if there's a strong colour contrast. Black and white's an obvious case; it can feel like one long hangover if you're not careful.

Where to use pattern

Of course how much impact you *want* a pattern to make depends on what room it's destined for. If it's the living room, where you're going to spend most of your time, beware of anything too strong or flamboyant. You'll feel it breathing down your neck at best; find it's driving you mad with irritation at worst. Go for a small all-over pattern that looks almost plain from a distance and save the big, bold designs for places you don't stay in long enough to feel dominated. The hall, for instance, is somewhere you can afford a striking pattern because all you're doing there is passing through it. So's the bathroom—and you have only yourself to blame if you soak in the tub long enough to feel the pressure. The dining room can take a demanding pattern too. Even if the novelty eventually wears off for you, dinner guests will be full of compliments as they receive their first impressions.

Another example of mixing patterns. This time the scale's tiny and unpretentious, with gingham wallpaper and smaller-gingham wall frieze co-existing peacefully with the flower-sprinkled bed-linen, curtains and roller blinds. Again, everything's kept simple.

In all these cases though, be prepared for your room to look smaller than if you'd 'stretched' it by keeping the walls plain. And accept that you won't be able to crowd it out with much in the way of furniture, pictures or bric-à-brac. These create patterns of their own, and to set them up in competition with large splashes of pattern elsewhere will only result in visual chaos.

Of course, it's not just pattern you need to consider when you finally get around to picking your wallpaper. Make sure you know what is meant by manufacturers' descriptions such as 'smearproof', 'washable' and so on (*7.1a). And avoid costly or even disastrous blunders through overestimating —or worse still, underestimating—how many rolls you are going to need (*7.1b). By the time you come to put it up, you may find it difficult to get a perfect colour-match, or the design may have been dropped from production.

A way of creating mood

Despite all these gloomy warnings, pattern is a vital part of decorating because it can do so many things. Firstly, it's an instant way of stamping a room with personality. Paste a William Morris-style paper on the walls and immediately you create a soft, romantic atmosphere; paste a cool, geometric paper instead

Pattern can be used to pull an awkward-shaped room together—and this dining room is about as awkward as you can get. Only possible solution is to apply an overall pattern that distracts attention from the irregularities and gives a semblance of unity. Here, a brave, swirly wallpaper covers all the walls and the corner cupboard. Matching fabric plays down the clumsily-positioned window with a roller blind and full-length curtains.

Sale, Stone & Senior; setting, Diana Austen

Another example of pattern pulling together an awkward situation. This time it's a hall full of faceless flush doors that made it look like a hospital corridor. Door-surrounds were painted white, panels of wallpaper to match the walls were pasted into position and finished with beading. Doors and walls now form part of an attractive whole.

and the result will be crisp and sophisticated. Secondly, it's a cheap way of 'furnishing' a room when you haven't got much furniture—it generates a warmth and 'busyness' that makes the place feel friendly and lived-in. Thirdly, it's much more practical than a plain surface that shows every mark. This is why patterned carpets are so popular in living rooms, but as they have a long life ahead of them try to pick a timeless and unobtrusive design.

Finally, pattern hides a multitude of sins by detracting attention from them. If a wall's lumpy and uneven, patterned wallpaper will hide the fact. If a room's full of awkward shapes and angles, an all-over pattern will pull it together in a unified whole. In other words, pattern makes a good servant but a bad master—and it's up to you to keep the whip hand.

8 CHOOSING THE
THE FURNITURE

Not many people can go out and furnish their homes in one go—and probably it's just as well. There's nothing so terrifying as complete freedom; a few financial limitations offer some kind of discipline to work to. They also force you to improvise and this often results in a far more individual and stimulating home than if you'd gone and bought up your local PERRINGS or HABITAT.

If you do have limitless money, you can make a conscious decision as to whether you want your home to be modern or traditional. But be warned: buying modern furniture (*8.1) can be a bit risky simply because what's modern today may look painfully dated in ten years time. Glass and tubular chrome steel tables are 'in' at the moment, but they could be as 'out' as 1950s splayed-legged tables before long. The secret lies in picking clean, basic shapes with a timeless appeal, the kind of furniture that'll be called 'classic' in the future. Or of course, picking modern classics that have already stood the test of time, like those shown on pages 62 and 63. They aren't cheap, but some of them are less expensive than 'contemporary' furniture, fussy with this year's details that'll look plain silly next year.

They aren't easy to use either. Unless you're very sure of what you're doing, modern furniture needs cool, modern surroundings. It demands a plain, almost stark background, which means you can't rely on pattern to distract attention from mistakes. And it demands plenty of space to give each item the kind of importance it deserves. What you leave out is almost more important than what you put in. And unless you get it just right, however near the miss, the result can look totally wrong.

Tolerant antiques

Perhaps that's why so many people prefer old or antique furniture. It's much less demanding, and you can go for a general effect instead of having to aim for cool perfection. It doesn't seem to mind being muddled together (like an English country garden, it often thrives on inspired disorder); it's happy to live with pattern and it looks just as good with strong, positive colours as soft, gentle ones. This is probably simply because it *is* old. It's developed enough warmth and character to survive most situations. Even if you mix periods of

1

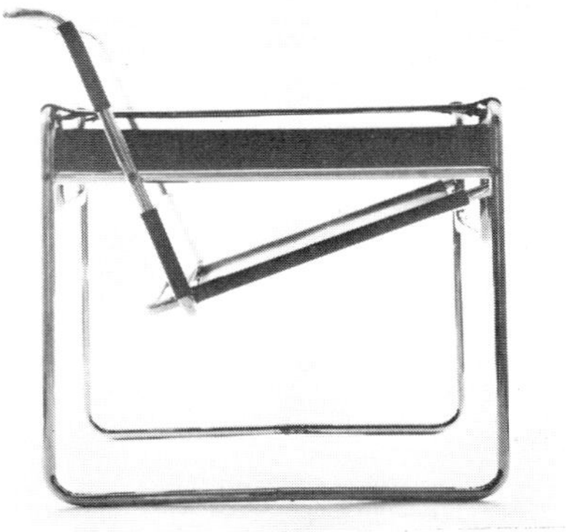

2

3

4

5

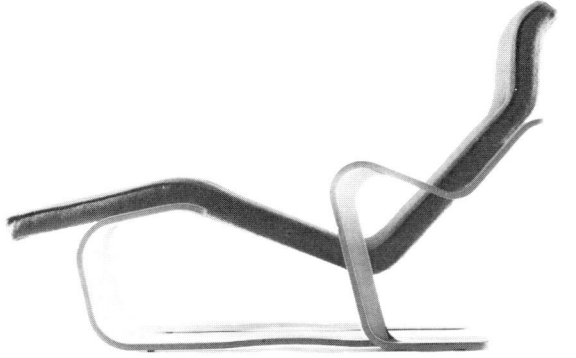

furniture (and being too purist could land you with a stiff museum-piece effect), the different shades of wood will all be mellow and in sympathy with each other. This richness creates its own sense of mood and unity, and almost guarantees that what you buy will look comfortably at home.

Of course, antiques aren't cheap, but unless you want posh collector's items they won't be any more expensive than the furniture that's being made today. And whether you buy them in shops, track them down in sale rooms or get left them by some lovely aunt, the only way they're going to date is by appreciating in value.

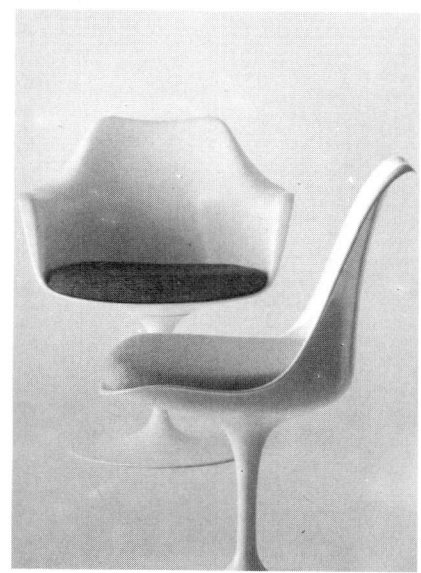

Opposite 1 *Wassily* chair designed by Marcel Breuer in 1925 comes in canvas or hide on a tubular frame. By and from FORM INTERNATIONAL. 2 *Barcelona* chair designed by Mies Van Der Rohe in 1929, upholstered in hide on a chromed mild steel frame. By and from FORM INTERNATIONAL. 3 Vertical steel rods combine with nicely rounded upholstery in Warren Platner's dining chair, designed in 1967. Made by FORM INTERNATIONAL and available from their showroom. 4 The *Bertoia* chair designed by Harry Bertoia in 1951. From the makers, FORM INTERNATIONAL. 5 *Isokon* chaise longue designed by Marcel Breuer in 1935 is made of bent beech and upholstered in pure wool or leather. From JOHN-ALAN DESIGNS. **Left:** Two versions of the *Tulip* chair, designed by Eero Saarinen in 1956. Available fixed or swivel from FORM INTERNATIONAL. **Below:** Lounge chair and ottoman designed by Charles Eames in 1956; moulded plywood on a cast aluminium frame, with down-filled leather upholstery. Made by Herman Miller and available from HEAL'S.

Anthony Blake

Anthony Blake

Making the best of what you've got

All very well if money's no object, but most of us build up our homes over the years and end up with a motley assortment of old and new. In many ways this is an advantage. All-modern rooms run the risk of looking like show houses; all-traditional rooms can look like theatre sets. This is why the majority of interior designers deliberately put something like an old oak chest in a room full of Italian plastic furniture, or sit EERO SAARINEN tulip chairs around an elegant Georgian table. It wilfully disturbs the balance and adds a spark that jolts the whole scheme into life.

So put your long, low modern coffee table in front of that Victorian chesterfield; fill your spanking new storage system with bits of old china; give those old bentwood chairs a lick of paint and sit them round your new ARKANA table. Provided they're all good of their type, they'll set-off each other and look better for the contrast.

Totally traditional drawing room in an 18th-century country cottage proves that clichés often are clichés because they *work*. But even so, wing chairs are upholstered in a hot orange-red that would have horrified the age of reason—and they're what sparks this potential museum-piece into life.

If they're not good of their type, you've got problems. (Moral: when you can't afford the best, forget second-best and choose an honest alternative.) All you can hope to do is integrate bad miscellaneous furniture with a common theme. If it's really hideous (and it often is when you're setting up home and making do with everyone's cast-offs) the safest treatment is to paint everything, walls, woodwork and furniture, neutral. This way even the most monstrous item will merge into its background, and if you drop in splashes of bright colour elsewhere (as described in Chapter 5), they draw attention away from faults still further.

If the shape of your furniture's reasonable, but the woods are a mad mixture that haven't been around long enough to develop a shared mellowness, paint all the furniture one strong colour. This creates a sense of unity, and if you want to emphasise it even more, try replacing all the handles you can with white china knobs. Then the similarities will hit the eye before the

Uncompromisingly modern living room teams glass, leather and chrome steel into a cool, sophisticated whole. Geometric carpet and abstract paintings provide the only pattern that's allowed—but out of picture, an old mahogany table softens the stark-as-a-showroom impression.

differences and it will take a long, cool appraisal to realise what you've been up to.

If the scale of your furniture's all wrong—this is something you can't avoid if you're furnishing with hand-me-downs, but do watch proportions when actually buying something (*8.2)—try to minimise different heights by containing various pieces within the same frame. In a bedroom, for instance, run an equal-in-depth shelf along the top of the highest item (probably a ward-robe) to stretch from wall to wall. Then drop down uprights to house, say, a chest and fill in gaps with shelving and an improvised dressing table. Finally, paint frame and contents to match, and you've got a neat and convincing run of 'custom-made' units.

Buying on a budget

Sometimes the best ideas come from the worst bank balances, so take heart if yours is sinking slowly into the red.

The cheapest way to furnish a home is with junk (*8.3)—not the pretty junk that's expensive nowadays, but the ugly junk that no one else is interested in. Just keep reminding yourself that basically, furniture's always the same. Each era adds on its 'contemporary' touches, but there must be opportunities for pruning them off sometimes. Train your eye to find the possibilities in the 50p pieces that other people dismiss as impossible. Given some inspired lopping, they can probably be adapted to the looks that are contemporary today.

New furniture from junk: In other words, don't spurn those dark-varnished 1930s sideboards with barley sugar legs, over-ornate backs and hideous handles. Saw off the legs and back, paint what's left white, add new handles—and you've got some compact wall-hung storage ready to mount in place. Similarly, don't turn your back on that vast mahogany tallboy that would dwarf present-day bedrooms, provided the drawers aren't warped. Oppressively big it may be, but it can easily be cut down to size for today's living by slicing it straight across the middle. Add new tops and you've got two low chest-cum-tables for either side of your bed.

You can be just as tough with any chest of drawers that's too large for comfort. These usually come with two small side-by-side drawers at the top, two larger drawers, one below the other and an even larger drawer at the bottom. Slice off the bottom drawer, top with chipboard and a long foam cushion, and you've got a storage-cum-seating unit. And of course, you've also got a chest of acceptable proportions, that can easily be prettied up with new brass handles if necessary.

Even pre-war three-piece suites are worth some ingenuity because, after carpets, comfortable seating's the most expensive item to buy. Look out for 1930s squat square suites: the shape's in fashion now and it's an easy one for the amateur to re-cover. Sagging springs may just mean the webbing has gone, but anything more radical means expensive treatment, so it's no longer going to be a bargain. Even so, it may be worth buying a hopelessly down-at-heel suite just for the sake of the separate seat cushions. If these are plump and luxuriously down-filled, re-cover them, and line them up along a slatted bench. If you've enough of them, hang them from a pole along the wall above for a comfortable back rest.

Drastic surgery

Post-war fireside chairs, the kind that came in with TV viewing, have possibilities too, despite their splayed legs. Sometimes it's possible to re-cover them, incorporating a skirt to hide the legs (though do make it a tailored one with inverted pleats, or the result will look nearly as dated as when you started). Alternatively, you can be ruthless and lop off the legs, sitting the legless pieces along a bench. Legs aren't always splayed, but wooden arms often tilt upwards at a self-conscious angle. See if it's possible to cut them off without weakening the basic frame. Then you'll be left with presentable seating units that can be pushed together, or used separately, on the same principle as today's more flexible seating.

As for dining-chairs, junk shops are full of them. They'll all be odd, of course, but a matching coat of paint will pull them together visually. Check they haven't got rickets before you waste your money buying them, but don't be discouraged if a previous DIY king has replaced sagging cane with an amateurish seat. If it's sturdy, just add a small cushion, covered in fabric to match your table-cloth, plus four matching tapes for tying to the chair legs.

Unexpected sources

You can afford to buy new—if you buy the unexpected. Learn to recognise when things meant for one purpose can be used equally well for another. Most people have realised that cane garden furniture makes a reasonably cheap alternative to living room furniture, but before you jump on that particular bandwagon, remember it creaks like a dog basket when you sit in it. And it isn't so cheap once you've had to buy cushions to make it comfortable. A better answer might be to turn to the canteen section of an office furnishing catalogue, and look for forms with slatted wooden tops. All they need is a length of foam, covered in a pretty print, to make a simple seating unit to go with a dining table or to line up along a wall.

Office catalogues are a mine of ideas by the way—flick through the pages and you'll find bentwood coat and hat stands; stove-enamelled steel shelving at ludicrously cheap prices; moulded polypropylene stacking chairs, the kind that look cheap and nasty in a laundrette context but striking and sophisticated in the home; and simple but sturdy reconditioned desks, with or without small drawers at the top. Just paint them, and you've got a cheap dining table. Cut down the legs too, and you've got a chunky coffee table that out-Conrans Conran.

A trip to any large store can be rewarding too. Consider the potential of wallpaper-hanging trestle tables, the kind that have pine as opposed to hard-board tops and wooden folding legs instead of metal. These usually live down in the do-it-yourself departments. If you seal the top with a clear lacquer, the wood mellows to a honey-tone and you've got a handsome, practical and cheap

It's impossible to say whether this converted cabin-trunk from the attic is modern or traditional—with its handsome brass fittings it would blend into any setting. Inside and outside are papered with a left-over roll of wallpaper—a bit fiddly to manoeuvre round the locks, but well worth the effort. Here, the trunk acts as a toy-box in a nursery, but differently wallpapered to suit its surroundings, it could just as easily make a sewing-box or a hall 'table'. (N.B. Not a coffee-table—there's nowhere for your legs.)

Sale, Stone & Senior; setting, Diana Austen

Whitewood's very adaptable. Leave it natural and add brass or white china knobs, and it's traditional. Paint it a suede colour and add bright pink chevron-stripes, as in this bedroom, and it's modern. Main point to remember: whitewood is a *soft* wood, so check for dents before buying—and protect it afterwards with three coats of clear lacquer if you're leaving it natural; three coats of paint if not. For a really smooth finish, sandpaper between each coat, paying special attention to edges of drawers.

69

dining table. Visit the whitewood department too. Whitewood furniture isn't cheap any longer, but it's still cheaper than conventional furniture, and lends itself to all kinds of interpretations. Page 69 shows one of them, suggests others, and explains just how much work is involved.

Solving your curtain problem

Finally do the rounds of the fabric departments and look for cheap non-curtain fabrics for curtains. Try bed ticking in subtle brown or charcoal stripes, soft and sheeny curtain lining in endless shades or unbleached calico, creamy-coloured, rough-textured and ideal for modern settings. Try pvc-treated printed cotton (*8.4) from the dress fabric department, the kind that's meant to be made into raincoats. Especially practical for curtains or roller blinds in the kitchen or bathroom, but so pretty they'll look good anywhere. Or buy cotton gingham, which can look fresh and unpretentious or neat and formal, according to how you use it. And if you're hopeless at sewing, buy felt (*8.5) that you simply cut to size and don't need to hem. It's a natural for curtains and bedspreads—and it comes in colours more vibrant than any other material can manage.

What you lack in money you must make up for in ideas—and you'll probably end up with a far more attractive home than your stinking-rich next door neighbour.

9 A PLACE FOR EVERYTHING

Once upon a time, houses had cellars and attics where everything from cabin trunks to stuffed foxes heads found a home. Nowadays if we're lucky enough to have them, we promptly convert them into extra living space. Great—except that we still have the cabin trunks and stuffed foxes heads, or whatever the equivalents are today. And what's more, we have to accommodate them in rooms much smaller than our grandparents would have expected the servants to live in.

This explains why storage is so vital a part of modern living. It's a way of containing our possessions so we're not falling over them all the time but know just where they are when we want them—in theory at any rate.

Of course homes have always had storage (like sex, it's not something this century has invented). But before it was mostly free-standing storage. You had a wardrobe, a dressing-table, a chest of drawers and a tallboy in your bedroom. You had occasional tables, what-nots and display cabinets in your drawing room to show off your ornaments. In other words—you had plenty of floor-space.

Try the same approach today and life would be one long obstacle race. Storage has had to go to the wall, leaving as much floor area free as possible, so we can move without collisions, and whizz over the carpet with the vacuum cleaner instead of manoeuvring round a maze of spindly legs.

How to confine your clutter
If you can possibly afford it, a wall-to-wall run of storage provides the least obtrusive way of confining all your clutter into a neat entity. Efficient systems (*9) aren't cheap, but they're so comprehensive they whittle down the amount of furniture you need elsewhere to an absolute minimum. In the living room for instance, a single wall could house your books, ornaments, plants, hi-fi, television, radio, drinks and glasses, writing materials (behind a flap-down front that acts as a desk) and unadulterated junk (preferably hidden behind cupboard fronts). Then all you'd need would be some seating units and a coffee table. Similarly in a bedroom one wall could house everything from dresses, suits, socks and pullovers to make-up drawers and a well-lit mirror, leaving nothing else to buy but the bed and a couple of bedside tables.

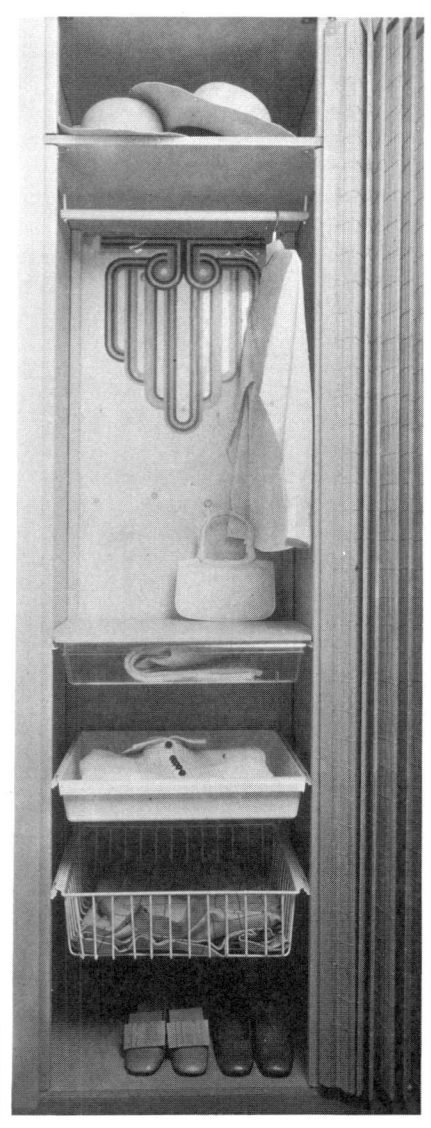

Bob Croxford

If you've got a handy alcove, put it to use as a wardrobe by building a timber frame to hang doors from. On the left, it's a solid-wood sliding door painted blue to match the interior woodwork and flower-patterned wallpaper. On the right, it's a natural rush concertina door to match the clear-lacquered wood, with only a stick-on transfer at the back to add pattern. In both cases, hanging drawers and baskets are by GRATNELLS. PS. SOLARBO FITMENTS make easily installed wardrobe components to fit any alcove.

You CAN take it with you

One advantage of wall-to-wall storage is that it can look built-in even when it's free-standing on the floor, or screwed to the wall so simply it can easily be dismantled. It isn't difficult to give this custom-built impression, because most good systems can be pieced together like a MECCANO set until they fill or nearly fill the length you require. Units based on a 100 mm (4 in.) module can't possibly leave more than a 125 mm (5 in.) gap at the end; even units based on a 550 mm (22 in.) module will only waste 200 mm (8 in.) along a 7-ft wall. And although heights vary, you can usually add top cupboards for an almost floor-to-ceiling result. When you're putting white units against a white wall, gaps are barely noticeable, especially if you install units from the centre of the wall and work outwards for perfect symmetry. But if you're a perfectionist, most manufacturers supply top and side scribing pieces that fill the gaps imperceptibly.

This type of storage is extremely flexible. For a start, you don't *have* to buy it all at once—you can build it up as finances permit. Then you can re-arrange however much you've managed to buy whenever you feel like it. Shelves, drawers, drink cupboards, writing 'desks', wardrobe hanging rails will all be adjustable; if they're not, buy a different system. Every home changes its storage needs and you're going to need units that can change with them. You may have a small television set at the moment, but next year you might buy a big colour set and then you'll need to move a shelf up several inches to accommodate it. Or you may move house altogether. Then you'll want to take your storage with you and put it together a different way to suit its new surroundings.

Leave it behind when you go

This kind of flexibility isn't possible with built-in storage—not without a lot of time and carpentry anyway. Even so, built-in storage has proved popular in the past because purchase tax wasn't charged on 'cupboard units and drawer units of the types which are supplied to house builders and which are incomplete until installed by the builder'. In other words, anything backless, sideless and topless was much cheaper, at least until VAT threw a spanner in the works. The major snag was, and is, that built-in storage isn't adaptable. There isn't the freedom to move individual units around and if you move house, the storage has to stay behind. This doesn't matter if you can add the cost of the storage to the purchase price of your house but problems arise when prospective purchasers already have free-standing storage that they're wanting to bring with them.

Choosing storage on a budget

So far so good—presuming you've got a healthy bank balance. But if it's only just managing to stay in the red, open shelving is the cheapest form of storage on the market. The main disadvantage, of course, is that all your belongings are on view, which is fine when it's a matter of plants and bric-à-brac but not so good when it's a tatty pile of bills or the dress you're half-way through making. A cheap solution here is to fix a roller blind to the top shelf and pull it down over your multitude of sins when the chaos gets unbearable. This'll cut down on the dusting too.

The most flexible form of shelving is the TEBRAX type (see page 68 for an example), where you fix metal uprights to the wall, slot in brackets at any height you like and simply place or screw your shelf on top. Least flexible (but much cheaper) is when you make bridging shelves to fit an alcove. A neat way of doing this is to fix battens to the side walls and sit or screw the shelf on top. Either way, timber is the best material, whether in the form of solid plank, plywood, veneered chipboard or blockboard; with the latter, make sure the core strips run the same direction as the shelf. Be wary of ordinary chipboard

If you can afford it, a system like STAG'S OPUS is ideal for a bedroom or living room, because you can carry it as far along the wall as you like, and alter the height of interior fitments to suit your needs. Here, for instance, hanging rails have shelves and drawers below, but if hemlines dropped, the components could easily be re-arranged. What's more if you moved house, you could move the whole lot with you.

This free-standing *Form Five* storage by G-PLAN packs untidy clutter behind its cupboard fronts and puts attractive clutter on display. Shelves, drawers and let-down flaps are adjustable, and if your wall's long enough, you can always add more units to take the television, hi-fi, and make a work-desk where you can sort out the family bills.

because it distorts under a heavy load and doesn't hold screws or nails very well.

REMPLOY industrial shelving, called *Lundia*, is comparatively cheap too (despite the advent of VAT). This is a free-standing system, with whitewood uprights drilled at 2 in. intervals, and whitewood shelves that hook into the uprights at whatever height you need them. In fact, you can get end panels, drawer units and cupboard fronts too in the REMPLOY system. Nearly as cheap, and more comprehensive system of storage, is the self-assembly KEWLOX *Lustre* range with sliding doors. Here, the doors are made of very handsome white-finished hardboard, which slot into neat metal uprights. While on the subject of budget buying, obviously the cheapest 'wardrobe' of them all is a hanging rail fitted across an alcove, a top shelf above (at least 1½ in. above the rail so the hangers come out without a fight) and a curtain across the front. And if you want interior drawers and sliding trays, GRATNELL's clear perspex fittings (see page 72) are some of the cheapest and most sophisticated on the market.

There's always room for a bit more storage—if you look hard for it. Here, narrow book-shelves fit happily into a 'useless' space. Another area that frequently gets wasted is the space above and around doors.

Putting a quart into a pint pot

The trouble with storage is that it follows Parkinson's Law. Junk exands to fill the space provided for it—especially as children grow up and start making their own contribution. This means you have to add storage in less obvious places—and if you look around you're sure to find a few.

Around the windows for instance. There's not much you can do with a window wall—it's usually too broken up for furniture and the space goes to waste. So why not build shelves all around the windows except immediately beneath, where you can make window seats with lift-up lids for extra storage. Fill the shelves with books and pretty things and replace the curtains with roller blinds so the result doesn't look to fussy; then cover the seat cushions and paint the shelf-uprights and underneath of the top shelves to match the blinds.

Or simply build shelves above a door, where again, space gets totally wasted. Or re-appraise the area underneath the stairs once the children get older and you can dispense with the pram. With intelligently-spaced shelves,

Clever way of creating more storage is to make it work in two directions. This is KANDYA'S *Peninsular* unit, looking as good from the dining room as the kitchen, and proving equally functional, because cupboards open from both sides.

it could store masses of items methodically, instead of just becoming a glory-hole where it's impossible to find anything.

Or try and use some of the vast volume of air space that gets wasted at the top of the stairs. This *is* more difficult to utilise and you'd have to be a very ambitious do-it-yourselfer to attempt the really strong structure that's required; but with access from the landing, it could be an ideal place for storing clean sheets and towels, if you don't have room elsewhere for a sensible linen cupboard.

Or try and make one lot of storage do double-duty for two rooms. Well, not so much rooms as room areas, because this is obviously most feasible in open plan situations. At the moment, many people choose a counter top to separate the kitchen area from the dining area. True it's easy to pass food across but it would still be easy if you had base cupboards opening from both directions, top cupboards ditto (held in position by sturdy floor-to-ceiling uprights) and a space between to act as a serving hatch. This would present a neat, almost solid wall (a major advantage if you don't have the time or inclination to keep your kitchen tidy) and give you normal kitchen storage on one side and 'sideboard' storage on the other. Expensive, but it's two for the price of one in terms of space as much as money.

Plenty of furniture, incidentally, does double-duty nowadays too. You can buy tables that swing open into bottle-holding segments, seats with bases that are really storage boxes, beds that have drawers underneath for spare blankets. Some of these border on gimmickry, so be realistic before you buy them. Do you really want a table-cum-drinks cabinet for instance, if someone's likely to ask for another Campari when the table top's covered with everyone else's filled glasses?

Getting the best from your storage

How much paraphernalia a storage unit can pack away depends not so much on how big it is but on how big a use is made of its capacity. The largest cupboard, inefficiently planned, can simply mean room for a good old rummage, while a smaller cupboard can hold just as much *and* have everything within easy reach. The secret lies in interior fittings—knowing which you need and where to put them. And to start you thinking along the right lines, here's a general guide on what to aim for.

Choose deep shelves for long items like sheets, but not for shallow items stored two-deep so that the front row falls out as you reach to the back. Again, choose deep drawers for fairly large items like pullovers, but not for small ones that will get flung upside down in the hunt for a single scarf. Space shelves widely apart for bulky items like blankets, but not for a tottering pile of light items that will collapse in a heap if you try to remove one. Make sure wardrobes are at least 600 mm (2 ft) deep; otherwise shoulders and sleeves of clothes will rub against the back wall and door and wear out more quickly. And check that you're making best use of your hanging space. If you've got a lot of skirts and blouses, why not use the wasted area below for another hanging rail that can take more short garments?

Keep all the things that you use regularly, or that you need both hands to tackle, within easy reach. When you're standing up, this is anywhere between 710 mm (about 2 ft 4 in.) and 915 mm (about 3 ft ½ in.) high. Lighter items that you can extract single-handed can come either lower or higher, say anywhere between 510 mm and 710 mm (1 ft 8 in. and 2 ft 4 in.) and 915 mm and 1320 mm (about 3 ft ½ in. and 4 ft 5 in.). As for items that are rarely used, put them right down the bottom or right up the top. You only need suitcases, for instance, from time to time, so it won't hurt you to crawl on all fours or stand on a chair for the odd occasion.

10 ADDING THE ETCETERAS

You've picked your colour scheme, you've handled your pattern, you've chosen your furniture, planned your storage—but you've *still* got boxes full of bits and pieces, or if you haven't, you'll soon accumulate them! Nearly all of us are hoarders at heart—and that means *you* if you can't throw away your first French primer, are determined to keep that pretty saucer even though you've just broken the cup, or can't resist buying an old picture frame and hunting for a print to go in it. It's junk, but it's what turns a house into a home more surely than a cat curled up in front of a fireplace. Because it's what gives a room personality and makes it 'grow' on people subtly, long after the obvious impact has worn off.

The trouble is, like pattern, personal paraphernalia can easily threaten to take over. You've got to control it and this means grouping it within self-contained areas instead of scattering it distractingly around. It also means choosing the areas carefully, so they relate to existing furniture and architectural features.

Make a definite pattern

So far so good, but unless you position your group to fit in peacefully with the rest of the room, it'll demand too much attention and spoil the equilibrium. Try to line it up with something—perhaps over a mantelpiece or sofa, or so it levels with the top of a door or window—keeping it roughly within their confines. You don't have to be too precise about this. The group can fall short of the sofa edges or extend over them, for instance. The thing to remember is that as long as everything looks intentional and the balance is right you'll get away with it.

Grouping is just as important for items that are free-standing. If you've been collecting something like fluted green glass vases (or even miniature traction engines—if your hobby's remotely attractive, get it on show), mass them tightly together on an occasional table, march them in a straight line down a shelf or sit them symmetrically on a mantelpiece. However you do it, make a *definite* pattern with them instead of dotting them around so they look fiddly and lose their impact.

Michael Boys

1 If you collect anything that's visually attractive, consider hanging it on your wall. Here it's stop-watches, but it could just as well have been old keys or strings of brightly-coloured beads. 2 Masses of books can cover a wall like wallpaper and provide just as much pattern. PS. for do-it-yourselfers. This shelving system consists of home-made floor-to-ceiling 'ladders', with shelves resting across rungs wherever required. **Below: 3 and 4** Bits and pieces look fiddly and irritating dotted around—neat and satisfying grouped tightly together—whether in an alcove or over an old pine chest.

Jessica Strang

Arranging your books

Even if you're not a hoarder, you're bound to have books, and how you arrange them depends on how many you've got. If it's a matter of a few dozen rather than a few hundred, be cautious about packing them tightly together. They'll form a solid 'wodge' of colour and weight, and unless you deliberately balance them with something as heavy, they'll overpower whatever's around them. Say you've got wall-to-wall storage units for instance. Break up the books with bric-à-brac and leafy plants, instead of creating an isolated and lop-sided impact. Though if you've got hundreds of books it's another story. Fill an entire wall with them (making sure the shelves can take it—books by the yard are *very* heavy). This way they'll create a rich and regular pattern like wallpaper, and at the same time make your room look mellow and relaxed.

All these etceteras depend on pattern for coherence—and they'll provide so much of it they'll demand plain surroundings. So extend the rule from the previous chapter. Make it a patterned carpet *or* patterned fabric *or* patterned wallpaper *or* patterned etceteras. Or put your bits and pieces back in their boxes until it's time to decorate again.

Where to find your pictures . . .

If you want to cover large areas of your walls, buying posters (*10.1) is the cheapest way of doing it. The next cheapest is to buy a print—but there are prints and prints. The least expensive are the mass-produced prints known as 'reproductions'—these work well for watercolours and drawings but not so well for oil paintings where the texture is lost. Here you simply buy them if you like them—they're not going to appreciate in value because there are too many of them.

Original prints: Lino-cuts, lithographs, engravings etc. are more expensive, because they're usually printed in limited editions and approved and signed by the artist. But if they are, they should go up in value as well as giving you endless pleasure.

Originals aren't as expensive as most people think. You can buy drawings or paintings for well under £20 at most art galleries—even cheaper if you cut out the dealer's profit and go direct to the artist. Your local college of art probably holds an exhibition of students' work at the end of each year, and as there's masses of talent around, why not go along and buy what appeals to you. Here again, it's a matter of simply buying what you like; with originals you have to spend a lot of money on an established artist to be sure of a financial investment.

Framing them: If you're not careful, framing can cost as much as your picture. So look for cheap old frames in junk shops—they look surprisingly good with modern prints. And if you want to relate your pictures to their surroundings directly, make your own mounts by pressing your prints down on to thick card pasted with well-mixed POLYCELL, trimming off all white edges, and mounting it on to a larger board covered with fabric, hessian, textured wallpaper or colour left over from your room furnishing (*10.2).

And how to group them

Say you've got a hotchpotch of pictures lovingly culled from junk shops and other sources. Don't hang them self-consciously apart, so they demand more attention than they can possibly merit, but pack them closely together to form a satisfying relationship. It's a confidence trick really; as long as the grouping's tight you can get away with murder. Half the battle's convincing people you know what you're doing, so take the plunge—mix the good with the bad, stick in the odd mirror—and play the whole thing by ear.

Keep reminding yourself it's the *general* effect you're after, so the arrangement of your bits and pieces comes over as coherently as a single large painting. Even if you're faced with a thoroughly mixed bag of shapes and sizes, you should be able to manage without banging too many unnecessary holes in the wall.

The secret lies in defining your perimeter (though as your confidence grows, you may prefer a less rigid approach to the 'guaranteed' one we suggest here). Decide on a square or rectangle, and hang the highest row of pictures so the top of the frames forms a neat line and lowest row of pictures so the bottom of the frames does the same. Then make sure the outer edges of the pictures form neat side-lines, and simply fill in the middle with whatever's left.

Of course, this thinking doesn't just hold good for pictures. You can hang almost anything on the wall, from horse brasses to fob watches, from china plates to bangles and necklaces, from butterfly collections to bunches of keys. Anything that's good to look at is grist to the visual mill.

11 HALLS THAT SAY WELCOME

Many people treat halls as somewhere you whizz through as quickly as possible—a kind of no-man's-land, a necessary link between rooms—a means to an end but nothing in their own right.

There's no excuse for this really, not even a financial one. Most halls are too small to take the clutter of furniture, so furnishing costs are going to be minimal. Ideally, of course, there should be a cupboard to hang coats in (and if we're talking of ideals, preferably it should have some form of heating to dry damp clothes), but few halls have room for this. As coats hanging from wall pegs don't look very pretty, try to train your family to hang their clothes up in their bedrooms as soon as they come in. Or if that suggestion provokes hollow laughter, buy a curly bentwood hat-stand that can carry several coats and still look attractive.

Remember you'll be staggering through the front door with full shopping baskets. Try to squeeze in a small table you can dump your load on (to say nothing of letters, car keys, library books, gloves) and a tiny chair you can collapse on while you sort yourself out. And do fix a mirror on the wall somewhere (*11.1). Not only will this make your hall look bigger, but you'll be able to check your appearance as you rush out to catch the bank, collect the children from school or get a loaf of bread before the shops shut.

Tough, practical floor coverings

Even though halls should be treated like self-respecting rooms, they *are* primarily a link between other rooms. That means they get more wear and tear than anywhere else in the house, so whatever you put on the floor must be hard-wearing. And as there are some people who'll always ignore the doormat (despite the fact that, ideally again, you've bought a large one and fitted it into a non-skid well) it'll need to be easy to clean. A top quality wool carpet in a medium-to-dark colour provides the most warm and welcoming solution; even a light-coloured carpet in a flat, where people have 'wiped' their feet walking up the communal stairs before they reach you. But alas, it's also the most expensive—and once you plump for carpet, you're really committed to taking it up the stairs and along the landing. Otherwise the result will look bitty and the break in continuity will make your hall look even smaller than it is. If you can't afford a really good carpet, don't waste your money on cheaper ones that will soon go shabby. Buy a tough woven jute or sisal floor-covering like *Tintawn*, that'll take all the punishment you can give it. It has a rough, masculine texture that provides plenty of visual interest, and comes in vibrant colours (though beware, the vibrance does fade if subjected to strong sunlight).

Rush matting or tiles? If you live in the country where people are going to be tramping in with muddy feet, or simply can't afford carpet, try rush matting. This looks warm and friendly, and when it gets filthy you can take it out into the garden, scrub it, and leave it to dry in the sun. Or try any of the easy-to-clean floorings that come in tile form. Vinyl or lino tiles are an obvious choice, and it takes a lot to beat the traditional black and white chequer

Most landings are bleak and impersonal because, like halls, impact has to be made through a bare shell of walls, floor and ceiling, without the help of furniture. Surest way to create effect is to pick a strong but simple colour scheme. Here, all-over mustard does the trick in a warm but subtle way; also smoothes out the crazy ceiling angles and 'loses' a door. Stark black and white floor tiles sharpen the result. But most important of all, horizontal band of paintings at eye height keeps people psychologically on the level and distracts attention from the ceiling above. Posters could be grouped in the same way.

pattern. But if you want something different, *Gerflex* tiles come ready cut in Moroccan tile shape—and of course, there's nothing to stop you laying plain tiles (*11.2) and making your own contrasting pattern or border.

Other tiles, like ready-sealed cork, are more expensive—but they're equally practical and even better to look at. Quarry tiles are virtually indestructible (it takes centuries to wear them down into a comfortable hollow). Although heels make quite a clatter on them, they're so handsome and subtly-coloured it doesn't seem to matter. The same applies to sanded-and-sealed wood floors, only more so. They look terrific, but two small children can sound like an advancing army.

Wooden stairs look good stripped too, but with children or old people in the home, it's safest to carpet them and avoid the risk of slipping. It'll save you a lot of dusting and re-painting if you can take the carpet right across the tread of the stair. However, unless you're very lucky, you'll find the 27 in. width is too narrow and the 36 in. width so wide that you'll have to cut it and waste the surplus.

Wall coverings must be durable

Walls need to be just as tough and practical, because people are going to brush against them as they come in the front door (so are wet, smelly dogs if you've got one) and kids are going to skid against them with their scooters. You're probably going to do some damage yourself if you keep a pram or pushchair in the hall.

This isn't the only consideration. Halls look best when the wall-covering is carried up the stairs and on to the landing, which means there's a very large and high expanse of wall to tackle. Balancing ladders on stairs or rigging up platforms on scaffolds is enough to daunt any do-it-yourselfer, but so are the prices professionals charge. Whichever way you take out of the dilemma, think very carefully before deciding what to put on the walls. There's going to be far too much effort and expense involved to waste on decorations that aren't going to be long-lasting.

Because halls are places you pass through, you can afford to use a patterned wallpaper (*7.1, 1a) that might send you potty in a living room. The more all-over and busy the pattern the better, as this will disguise any marks. Washable wallpapers have a fine, protective coat that can be gently wiped clean, so they're a more sensible choice than standard wallpapers. Obviously the *most* sensible choice is a vinyl wall-covering that's scrubable but patterns still leave a lot to be desired, and plain vinyls often have a silky finish that's going to look cold and unfriendly if you team it with a hard, polished floor.

Unless you can carry it off with real panache, gloss paint looks miserably chilly with anything but carpet or rush matting, as well as showing up every fault in the plastering. Emulsion, though much warmer, is not very practical. If you need to soften a wall with warmth and texture, hessian (*8.5, 12.6) is long-lasting enough to still any pangs of guilt about the price and it hides dodgy plasterwork. The natural colour is surprisingly dirt-disguising, and if you buy paper-backed *Canotex*, when it eventually loses the battle against grime, you can keep the texture but add some colour by over-painting it with emulsion.

Stick to the rules

Halls and stairways can take a lot of pattern, but don't get too carried away with the idea. If you've decided on a patterned carpet, for instance, pick a fairly small-scale design that repeats itself neatly and logically. This will make the floor area look larger and make walking down the stairs much safer, because with a large, rambling pattern, you won't be able to tell where one tread ends and another begins. (Efficient lighting helps here. Keep it clear and central. Recessed downlighters are the ideal both for stairs and halls; so are spot-lights, that can be angled to throw light just where it's needed.) And remember the rule about having either patterned carpet *or* patterned wallpaper in Chapter 7. It's a rule that can be broken if you're very sure of yourself, but by and large, it's better to play safe and settle for one or the other.

It's also best to keep window treatments simple. Unless you've got a large hall, complicated drapes are going to have a swamping effect. Consider neat roller blinds instead—in fact, consider nothing if the windows are small and not too overlooked.

This doesn't mean plain walls with self-effacing windows need be dull. Because there's so little room for furniture in halls and on landings, there's every excuse for turning back to Chapter 10 on handling the etceteras and deciding how to provide interest on the walls. If you can afford to lose 6 in. of through-space in this busy traffic area, fix narrow shelves and display your books and bric-à-brac; if you can't, arrange pictures or collections in self-contained groups at eye-level height. This will stamp your home with your personality as soon as people walk into it, and give a good first impression to everyone—including the postman.

SPECIAL PROBLEMS

The hall is sometimes the most awkward space of all to know how to handle. Here are a few suggestions for tackling problems commonly found in old houses and flats.

Too many doors: If you've got a hall with so many doors leading off it looks like a hospital corridor, give them the same treatment that you give the walls and they'll become an integral part of them. This works so well with patterned wallpaper or fabric (see page 60), that unless you choose distinctive door knobs, you run the risk of getting lost in your own home.

If you don't like being surrounded by pattern, an alternative solution is to make a virtue of necessity and turn the doors into an attractive feature. (This is something you may *need* to do if your hall lacks natural assets but is so long and narrow that furniture can't come to the rescue.) In this case, re-appraise the meagre basics—the doors, architraves, skirting boards and if you're lucky enough to have it, ceiling coving. Choose a plain but possibly textured wall covering for the walls and carry it over the panels of the door

86

(page 60 shows how easy it is to fake panels if you don't have any). Then find a deep but complementary colour, and paint the rest of the doors, architraves, skirting and the coves. Finally, pick out the beading on the doors, the knobs, the edges of the architraves and skirting boards and the edge of the coving, with a bright accent colour.

This will create a meticulous frieze pattern—and all you'll need is a mirror and some pictures (frames or mounts carefully co-ordinated), to make your basically bare hall look fully furnished. The most successful example we've seen had olive and white chequer-patterned vinyl tiles on the floor, natural grasspaper on the walls and door panels, deep olive paint on the remaining woodwork, plus a brilliant turquoise for picking out the edges. Very sophisticated, but if it sounds too elaborate for your tastes or budget, simply strip doors, architraves and skirting boards back to the wood, seal them with a clear lacquer and you'll have a natural and easy-to-live-with pattern.

Lowering a high ceiling

If you've got a hall that's not only long and narrow, but dauntingly high, bring the ceiling down to human dimensions. If you can afford it, the simplest way is to build a false ceiling—something that gives you the chance to incorporate recessed lighting. This is expensive, but there are cheaper ways if you're prepared to be ingenious. For instance, why not fix a row of hooks along both walls, about 1 ft 6 in. apart and about 1 ft 3 in. above the doors. Then beginning at one end, tie white nylon cord to the first hook, carry it across to its opposite number, run it along the wall to the next hook, then back across the hall to its opposite number and so on to the far end. This'll give you a simple frame on which to loop a roll of white cartridge paper (available in long lengths to order from most big stationers) or a roll of light fabric (provided you dyed the nylon cord to match first).

Start at one end of the hall and staple the paper or fabric directly on to the far wall. Then loop it over the cord so each loop hangs down about 1 ft (high enough to clear the doors), nipping the paper or fabric together and stapling it just under the cord each loop rests on. If you've used fabric, you may have to arrange some form of wall-fixed lighting. But if you've used paper, provided lights are ceiling-fixed and high enough for safety, the paper will diffuse the light so the hall is bathed in a soft, white glow. This works especially well in a hall that has no natural light.

Treatment for a narrow hall

If that sounds too much like hard work, use a few visual tricks to make the hall *look* wider and lower, without actually changing its shape. Choose a carpet with horizontal stripes that'll 'stretch' the floor area widthways. Or buy sheet vinyl in two plain colours, get to work with a STANLEY knife, and alternate wide expanses of one colour with narrow, horizontal stripes of another. Or break the walls up visually so they're not as high and imposing. One way is to make an old-fashioned dado (the example on page 15 shows

Halls get tramped through more often than any other area, so they've got to be tough enough to take it. Here, walls are stripped back to the original pine panelling, so the odd scrape with a scooter only adds character. Floor and stair carpet is in sturdy sisal; keeps to sober brown to disguise dirt, and to complete a neutral shell that bright colour can be dropped into. This comes with a modern painting (the kind that's ideal for making impact when you're just passing through—but might drive you mad in your living room). Also with the visual jigsaw of posters and kids' paintings. These do get ripped at floor-level by the three children of the household, but posters are cheap and easy to replace.

painted matchboard—but if you're hopeless at carpentry, you could paper the bottom three feet of the wall with a traditional-patterned *Anaglypta* and finish it off with beading). Another way is to form panels that keep the interest at eye-level; although the picture on page 89 shows a living room, the wall treatment would transfer to a hall with the greatest of ease.

Of course, if your hall is dark and gloomy even on the sunniest day, simply hanging a row of *low* pendant lights along the ceiling and keeping them on continually could do the trick. They'll flood everything below them with light—and the cavernous ceiling above will recede into obscurity.

12 WHERE THE LIVING IS EASY

Once upon a time every living room had a fireplace. In winter, people sat round it till their ankles mottled with the heat; in summer people still sat round it, probably gazing at a display of dried flowers. They may not have had the even heat that central heating brings, but they did have what so many living rooms lack today—a focal point.

One way of furnishing a living room on a budget; splurge nearly all your money on fitted carpet and survive with the minimum of furniture till you can afford more. Carpet will make the room *feel* fully-furnished; stylised wall treatment will make it *look* fully-furnished. Here, panels of bright-coloured stripes take the bareness off the walls and carry right through the curtains too. They may not be the kind of thing you want to live with forever, but when you finally acquire more furniture, they're easily discarded, and the neutral carpet will give you a free hand for deciding on a permanent colour scheme.

Sale, Stone & Senior; setting, Diana Austen

Finding a focal point

There's nothing quite so dispiriting as an aimless arrangement of furniture. It suggests a lack of permanence and security, so even if you don't have a fireplace—and plenty of people with central heating are having non-operational ones installed nowadays—(* 12.1), pick on *something* to group seating around in a definite and self-contained way. In most cases this will be the television set, but don't perch it, wires trailing, on a low table placed at a twee angle across a corner, drawing the rest of the furniture to it like a magnet. Television sets are unobtrusive at best, hideous at worst and not up to providing an attractive focal point either way. All you can do is make them part of a much larger and worth-looking-at focal point. The simplest way is to confine them (along with other equipment such as radios, record players, speakers etc.), into a good-looking run of storage that has plenty of plants and bric-à-brac to provide colour and interest. Then once everything's centralised in this way, seating can fall logically into position. Not in a long line facing the storage-wall of course, but making a positive, tight-knit shape.

Arranging the furniture

In a small room, sofa or pushed-together seating units can face the focal point from up against the opposite wall, perhaps with pictures above. Armchairs or seating units down the side wall can face into the focal point, ideally with a square coffee table to form the corner of the logical L-shaped arrangement. However in a larger room, seating will look as self-conscious as a dentist's waiting room ranged up against the walls. Far better to group it round one big coffee table in the centre of the room, perhaps with two facing settees or one settee facing two armchairs.

Obviously these cut-and-dried suggestions will need adapting for different circumstances, but generally the approach stays the same. Go for compact groupings of furniture that look intimate and intentional, instead of scattering items around so sparsely they look bleak and lost. This makes special sense if your living room has to be multi-purpose. As we saw in Chapter 2, some members of the family may want to relax and watch television, others may want to sit and sew or read, the children may want to do homework or start sticking an aeroplane kit together and in an open-plan living-dining room, everyone's going to have to eat meals there as well.

Define areas with lighting

In this situation, use lighting (* 12.2) to define your separate groups of furniture still further. Hang a low pendant light over the dining area, so it's held in its own self-contained pool of light. Put a standard spot-light beside the sewing/reading area, or fix an adjustable spot-light to the wall, so light can be angled just where it's needed and won't spill over to anywhere else. And if homework or bill-paying gets done at a desk unit within your run of storage, fix a spot or adjustable angle lamp to the back of the unit or the wall, so that whoever is working gets a private source of light. Then all that remains is to provide subtle lighting for the main seating area—perhaps wall-brackets with shades, or a white rice paper lantern hanging low over the coffee table to diffuse light softly.

Choosing the flooring

If you're working to a strict budget, there are two ways of choosing flooring for a living room. Either give it top priority and economise on furniture or splurge nearly all your money on luxurious and comfortable seating. You'll have to be fairly young and flexible to do it the first way. Top quality wall-to-wall carpeting (*12.3) *does* give a room an instantly furnished and luxurious look (see page 89 for an example), but sitting on jumbo-size cushions isn't very comfortable unless you're a practising yogi. Of course, the carpet must be top quality. Living rooms get so much wear and tear (they're classified as 'heavy traffic areas' along with halls) that it's pointless 'economising' with a cheap bedroom-quality carpet that'll look worse than a rag within a few months. If you're putting the emphasis on carpet, make sure it's long-lasting and also that you're going to be happy to live with it for several years. Obviously plain, neutral carpet's the most adaptable and easy-to-live-with but if you've got young children spilling orange juice, or a dog that leaves a trail of muddy paw marks behind it, choose any all-over pattern that's not too distracting. Unless your room's enormous, make sure it's not too large-scale either, because the pattern will 'shrink' the floor area and once furniture's in position, you won't even be able to 'read' the design either.

Alternatives to carpet: If you can't afford *good* carpet, forget it completely and go for something different. If your basic floor is smooth and even, lay vinyl or cork tiles (*12.4) or cover it with natural rush matting. Or if the boards are in good condition, sand and seal them (*12.5) to a warm, tawny colour, or paint them with a tough polyurethane paint—provided you keep the tin handy for touching up scuff marks. Then all you need is a rug to soften the effect, which can be put between your facing or L-shaped seating to give extra definition to the group. Shaggy long-pile and goatskin rugs provide texture if you need it; oriental rugs provide pattern and are much cheaper than most people think.

Laying a sub-floor: If your floorboards are ragged, uneven and shrunk so there are wide gaps between them, there's nothing for it but to lay a sub-floor before you consider laying anything on top. Try sheets of hardboard; once they're tacked down, you may decide they look good enough to face the world on their own, sealed with a coat of clear lacquer for protection, which accentuates their grainy-texture. Again, you'll need a rug for a splash of luxury but the result will look nearly as good as much more expensive cork tiles. And when you can afford decent carpet, the rug can go upstairs to a bedroom and you'll have a good, sound sub-floor that'll make whatever goes on top longer-lasting. By the way, never fall for display felt, however thick and brilliantly-coloured. It shows every piece of cotton and fluff, it won't respond to a vacuum-cleaner and you'll have to crouch on all fours picking bits up individually.

What to put on the walls

Most living rooms look best with an all-over coat of emulsion. This may sound uninspired, but if you've got storage filled with bric-à-brac along one wall and a patterned rug on the floor, you're not going to need patterned wallpaper competing with it. At all events, steer clear of any very demanding pattern. You're going to be seeing an awful lot of it, and it could start irritating you within weeks of its arrival.

If the walls are in bad condition, and you can't face the upheaval of re-plastering, cover them with something textured like hessian, felt (*12.6), cork or grasspaper. These are all much more practical than they sound, and they'll give your room warmth and character in a way that makes you, and your guests feel welcome.

Proving we practise what we preach, this living room belongs to the Editor of *Good Housekeeping*. Two sofas are grouped tightly round a rug to form a well-defined conversation area, and face a positive focal point made up of storage. Television fits discreetly under the bottom shelf when not in use, and colours keep to restful shades of brown. Here, the rug sits on expensive fitted carpet, but on a budget, you could spend most of your money on furniture and sit a rug on polished or painted boards instead.

13 GOOD EATING PLACES

If you're lucky enough to have a dining room, make the most of it. It's not a room you're going to spend long periods in—well, there are times when you and your guests will prop yourselves up on your elbows and go on talking and drinking endless cups of coffee into the small hours—but generally

Simple budget dining room, where mustard on the walls does most of the 'furnishing' by making the place look warm instead of bare. Rush matting on the floor is cheap but friendly; battered old table gets a floor-length mustard felt cloth (overlaid with white at mealtimes) to hide the scars. Sideboard (the bottom half of a dresser so damaged nobody else wanted it) is painted white with a new pine top added, and cheap junk-shop mirror looks expensive with a lick of paint.

speaking, it's never used for more than an hour at a stretch. This means you can throw caution to the winds and take risks you wouldn't dream of taking elsewhere. You can use strong colour (though think twice about anything like purple—it's a bit much with meat and two veg.). You can use flamboyant pattern because you won't be there long enough to get tired of it; you can go in for elaborate window treatments that would seem theatrical if you lived with them all the time.

Being realistic about furnishings

Although carpets are quiet and luxurious in a dining room, muffling the scraping back of chairs and all your to-ing and fro-ing from the kitchen, they're not really practical. This is true even if you haven't got babies flinging their food from high chairs, or children who make more crumbs from a piece of cake than you ever thought it had in it. Even at the most elegant dinner parties, some adult's bound to drop a pea on the floor and proceed to tread it in, or knock over a glass of wine while expansively illustrating an anecdote. And why not? People must be able to relax and enjoy themselves while they're eating and the surroundings you provide for them have simply got to be able to take it.

This is why all the practical floor-coverings we've mentioned in previous chapters make sense here: polished wood floors, sealed cork tiles and—if you're sure you're not going to drop the best china—quarry or ceramic tiles. Lino and vinyl can look particularly good too. It's a mistake to see them only in a kitchen context; team black and white tiles with rich Regency furniture, for instance, and they'll look formal and elegant instead of dull and sensible.

Unless your dining table's right up against the wall, you can choose hopelessly impractical wall coverings like fabric which will deaden the sound of clashing cutlery too. Felt looks especially rich and warm, and comes in a range of colours so vibrant they glow like jewels. But make sure your dining room is efficiently ventilated first: fabric tends to retain cooking smells, and last week's onion is never very appetising. Otherwise, it's back to your washable wallpapers and vinyls, though you can use a standard wallpaper if you give the area near the table a protective coat of transparent *Gard* or *Fend*. Or back to paint of course. Here emulsion looks the warmest, and you can simply re-paint the table wall when someone splashes it with gravy.

Dining in the round

Dining rooms demand very little furniture. All you need is a table, some chairs and a sideboard, or something to act as a sideboard. If you can possibly afford the space, buy a round table. It's best for conversation (if you get stuck opposite someone dull at a rectangular table, you've practically had it for the evening, but you can always talk around or across a circular table without much difficulty) and it provides the room with a round, satisfying shape. It also takes more people in less space—though ideally, leave as much as 2 ft for each place setting. This means you need a 4 ft-diameter

94

table for six people and a 5 ft-diameter table for eight people.

Beware of cramming a circular table into too small a room. It may fit all right with the chairs tucked tidily underneath, but once a chair's full of person, it sticks out about 1 ft 9 in. from the table and you're going to need at least another foot to be able to squeeze past it. In other words, your dining room must be at least 9 ft 6 in. square before you can contemplate a 4 ft-diameter table—and even then, the door will have to open outwards. Much better to have a rectangular table if you're in doubt—and if you're really pushed for space, use benches instead of dining chairs, because they don't have any legs to stick out.

Dining tables with matching chairs are expensive, often rather staid and boring too. If you're setting up home on a rock-bottom budget, do what we suggested in Chapter 8, and buy a cheap wallpaper trestle table. The wood can be sealed for a handsome and practical finish, and you can team it with cheap junk shop chairs painted a bright colour so they 'match' each other even if they're a strange assortment of shapes. Or hunt around junk shops for any old table that's got sturdy legs (making sure they *are* sturdy, or you'll curse every time you start carving the Sunday joint). It doesn't matter how many dents and stains it's got on the top. Cover it with a pretty table cloth and no one will know what's underneath. If the legs are scuffed and ugly make it a floor-length cloth that stays put all the time and add an overcloth for meal times.

Conventional sideboards take up a lot of floor space for the amount of storage they provide and they're not particularly good-looking. You might be better off with wall-fixed storage, where open shelves can provide a putting-down and serving surface, and display pretty things like china (*13.1); drawers and cupboard units can take cutlery and not-so-pretty things. Or if you need something traditional to soften a stark interior, a Welsh dresser might solve all your problems. Certainly no one has yet thought of a more decorative way of combining cupboards, drawers, open shelves, and a flat serving area.

Food on the move

Trolleys are a good idea if you've got room to wheel them around, because you can load all the dirty dishes on in one fell swoop and whizz them into the kitchen. Pay a little extra to get easy-running orbital castors though— otherwise they'll proceed as erratically as the trolleys in the local supermarket. Are serving hatches a good idea? Estate agents always mention them as if they're God's gift to housewives, and so they might be if there was a willing helper on the other side ferrying the food to the table. But usually there isn't, and unless there's a handy putting-down-cum-serving-surface beneath the hatch in the dining room (a hinged, flap-down shelf could do the job if space is short) it's merely a hole in the wall that the children yell through.

Obviously you need good lighting over your serving area (something a spot-light will provide in a simple and dramatic way), but elsewhere the lighting can be soft and romantic. In fact it needs to be for entertaining,

Grand but still budget-minded dining room, with a dramatic black wall setting the scene. Formally elegant curtains are made of cheap cotton gingham; the classically cool table-top is made of Melamine, not marble. Bright red cushions and table napkins bring warmth to a stylised setting that wouldn't be complete without its silver candelabra.

because it relaxes the atmosphere and encourages conversation between guests who may not have met before. Candles are the traditional answer for special occasions, whether they're long, tall ones in magnificent candelabra, or groups of nightlights, massed tightly together in foil baking trays for a lovely tinny glitter. Provided you can see to eat your food by them, they add an instant glamour that even manages to make Woolworth glasses sparkle.

For everyday occasions as well as entertaining, a pendant light fitting hanging low over the table creates nearly as intimate a mood. The bottom of the light fitting should be about 18 in. from the table. This height contains the table-top in a pool of light (dirty dishes stacked elsewhere fade discreetly into the shadows) and because it's just below face level, throws a flattering upward light that takes ten years off any woman's age. Final thought: make sure the pendant has a rise and fall device, which allows it to go up and down as easily as a roller blind. Then when your family's vanished from the table or your guests have gone home suitably impressed, you can zoom the light fitting up a few feet and clear away the coffee cups without cracking your head on it.

14 KITCHENS UNLIMITED

Kitchens are very personal places. Some people like them small, streamlined and efficient; others like them large, rambling and cosy. Some people like to toil over a hot stove in privacy; others like to chat away as they prepare a meal.

At the moment it's very fashionable to have an open plan kitchen, or at least a kitchen big enough for informal meals to be eaten in. Don't let yourself be brainwashed into this unless you're a natural, relaxed cook. Some people *need* to curse and mutter over their cooking like one of Macbeth's witches (and then switch to a serene Lady Macbeth as they cross the threshold into the dining room). Come to that, some people are so disorganised, they need to shut a door on the chaos they've left behind them.

How to plan a kitchen

There are three basic shapes to work from when planning a kitchen: I, L or U. The I-shape is for passage or galley kitchens where everything has to be fitted into a long, narrow room. Here, it's safest to put everything along one wall in a long thin line, starting with the sink and progressing from fridge to preparation area to cooker to workspace, and finally to serving area. If you think you've got room to put equipment along both walls (and you need at least 42 in. between units if cupboard doors aren't to crash into each other—alternatively you need sliding doors) make sure you keep the sink and cooker on the same side.

The L-shape: This is probably the best arrangement for a rectangular room. Kitchen experts talk about 'a work triangle' and this is the beat you pound between fridge, sink and cooker. Unless you need the exercise, the ideal distance is 14 ft in all, so try and bear this in mind when you position them. It's a good idea to start with the corner unit and work outwards from it, remembering that odd-sized walls can always be filled in with extra work-top space. A neat arrangement could be fridge, work-top, sink, corner unit plus extra allowance for preparation space, cooker, serving area. This could adapt quite easily to an open plan scheme if the shorter run was made up of a peninsular unit (*14.1), dividing kitchen from dining or living area.

The U-shape: This makes most sense in square kitchens, provided doors and windows don't foul up the best-laid plans. Possible layout could be: preparation area including fridge up one side to corner, large sink, corner, then cooker, centred with work area on one side and serving area on the other. (Again, one 'wall' could comprise a peninsular unit in an open plan situation.) Don't try and put a table in the middle unless there's at least 33 in. free all round it, or people will get wedged in so tightly, they'll have to play musical chairs to get themselves a glass of water.

All these basic shapes adhere to what the experts call 'a logical work sequence' which is simply a way of arranging things so you don't have to keep doubling back on your tracks. It applies to self-contained and open plan kitchens equally, so here's the theory even if you choose to ignore it. Basically, you should aim for four separate work areas: preparation, cooking, serving and washing up. Ideally, place preparation areas either side of the cooker, or between cooker and sink; plan the serving area near where you're going to eat, beside or beneath a hatch to the dining room or across a peninsular unit that divides the cooking area from the eating; allow enough space in the washing up area for dirty dishes to be piled up neatly out of the way.

Chaos and cracked hips

Until recently, there was nothing very logical *looking* about even the most logical work sequences. Kitchen unit manufacturers stolidly made their units 21 in. wide, whereas kitchen appliance manufacturers blithely went on making cookers and washing machines etc. several inches wider. (According to the British Standards Institution, 'wide' means how far the unit stands out from the wall, i.e. what we used to call 'deep'. As for what we'd formerly have called 'width', this is now known as 'length'. Presumably if we *all* adopt these terms, we'll know what we're talking about.) This confusion in makers' standards meant even the best-planned kitchen had a 'stepped' look to it, and even the most cautious cook usually ended up with at least one crack on the hip before the day was out. Some unit manufacturers managed a half-hearted tie-up with appliance manu-facturers—if you bought their units someone else's oven and hob unit could be built into it. But even so, unless you bought a continental system like BEEKAY-BAUKNECHT, where the same manufacturer made not only the units but the cookers, cooker hoods, ovens and hobs, dishwashers, fridges, freezers and washing machines, you hadn't a hope of getting an off-the-peg streamlined result. You either had to have the units custom-built to fit your equipment, or add false 'filling pieces' to the back of ready-made units, so they stood out farther from the wall and presented a united front.

Aiming for perfection

With luck (and it's going to need some luck, the way kitchen appliance manufacturers are dithering and bickering) the change to metric should improve the situation. Most unit manufacturers have jumped at the chance of a standardised system and started making units to the BSI's recommended

98

dimensions: height of work-top, 900 mm (36 in.); width—what we'd formerly have called depth—600 mm (24 in.); and length—what we'd formerly have called width—based on increases of 100 mm (4 in.), and usually available in 400, 500, 600 and 800 mm sizes. This means that you can permutate them to fill any wall to within 100 mm or less.

It remains to be seen whether appliance manufacturers will start making their products to fit these dimensions. But even if they miss this heaven-sent opportunity, the increased width of units must mean that cookers and washing machines will stick out less—in some cases as little as 50 mm (2 in.). And doubtless more unit manufacturers will give up waiting and do what HYGENA have done with their 2000 range, get a full range of appliances made on the continent (in their case, two sizes of built-in fridge, a washing machine, dishwasher, electric hob and oven, two types of cooker hood and an electric slicing machine), so that everything will automatically fit to perfection.

For the time being, some unit manufacturers are producing units to the old British imperial measure as well as the new metric system. If you're starting your kitchen from scratch, be sure to buy metric, because the imperial system is going to be phased out gradually, and should only be bought if you're filling gaps in an existing kitchen. Above all, don't be confused by the fact that imperial systems have started expressing themselves in metric terms. All they're doing is making a straight conversion from inches into millimetres—not working to the 100 mm metric module on which everything will be based in the future.

Choosing a cooker

Most people buy free-standing cookers in this country, probably for the very good reason that they're a lot cheaper than split-level ovens and hobs (which get even more expensive when you have to pay for a housing unit to take them). So far, none of the cooker manufacturers seem to have heard of the metric module—they're still making cookers in a motley assortment of sizes that make the chances of alignment with 600 mm wide units remote. (Continental firms like AEG, BOSCH, NEFF, SIEMENS and BEEKAY-BAUKNECHT, seem to be the only ones offering 600 mm wide and 900 mm high gas and electric cookers in this country and even then, you probably have to visit a good London retailer like Heal's to find salesmen who've heard of them.) In other words, with these exceptions, if you want a perfectly-fitted kitchen you're going to have to have a split-level arrangement or lump it.

Of course, split-level cooking has many advantages once you've got over the shock of how much it costs. Because the oven is sited at waist-level, you don't have to bend down to lift out heavy casseroles—quite something if you're pregnant or suffer from back trouble. And because the hob is separate from the oven, there's nothing to stop you having a gas hob, which will give you quicker, more controlled heat for things like sauces, and an electric oven which will give you much cleaner heat. This could prove a useful combination if the power strikes that are threatened every winter materialise.

Finally, there's more flexibility with split-level cooking. You can save energy by keeping the hob near the sink, and site the oven away from the work sequence near the serving area. But the main disadvantage is that small kitchens don't have the room to spread one function over two areas. It's fatal to squeeze in an oven and hob so tightly that there's no putting-down space either side of them.

New developments: Despite the fact that manufacturers haven't come to terms with metrication, there have been lots of new developments recently. Like self-cleaning ovens that can carbonise months of treacly deposits to a fine ash within minutes. (Self-cleaning, by the way, is not to be confused with continuous cleaning; this is a much cheaper but less efficient process, where a catalyst in the walls of the oven oxidises grease and helps prevent deposits from forming in the first place.) Like fan ovens, where a fan at the back circulates *even* heat in place of the usual uneven heat from elements at the sides. This reduces meat shrinkage, cuts electricity bills, and means food

Thoroughly modern kitchen, with gleaming HYGENA units and streamlined appliances. (Note the dropped-in sink top that allows the work surface to carry through unbroken.) Vinyl-tiled floor incorporates a Greek key design to relieve starkness, and this gets repeated in the practical roller blinds. Moulded stool by OMK DESIGNS.

straight from the freezer thaws and cooks consistently. Nearly all cooker manufacturers are making fan ovens now—and as they don't cost any more than conventional models, it's madness not to buy them. And like microwave ovens, which *do* cost more than ordinary ovens—but can roast a 4 lb joint of beef in 20 minutes and bake an apple in 8 minutes. This is because the process of converting microwaves to heat takes place *inside* the food as well as outside, so the food cooks all at once instead of having to wait for heat to penetrate. Obviously this is ideal for thawing and cooking food straight from the freezer; also for pre-cooking evening meals in the morning, because it only takes 2 minutes to heat them up, so there's no time for dehydration. Only snag with such speed: food cooks so quickly, there's not enough time for some items to brown. Roast chicken tends to look anaemic, for instance, and cakes don't acquire their usual crunchy top.

So much for ovens, but there's a new look in hobs too—one that'll appeal to you specially if you're in the habit of letting pans boil over. It's the ceramic hob, where a completely flat and easy-to-clean surface only heats up in the 'ring' areas but stays cool enough elsewhere for you to leave a tea-towel on the top without it scorching. Price is higher than for conventional hobs—but when you're not actually cooking, at least you've got a free pastry board! Finally, there are the many 'extra' appliances that can make you a quicker and more versatile cook, like wall-mounted rotisseries, plug-in saucepans and deep-fat fryers.

Picking a sink

If you can possibly scrape up the space and money for a double-drainer sink, buy one. It'll give you room for stacking dirty dishes on one side and draining them on the other. Stainless steel (although it *does* stain and soon gets scratched to a non-shiny surface) is much more practical than vitreous enamel (which chips), fireclay (which cracks *and* chips), and moulded plastic or perspex (which soon scratches and loses its bright, glossy look). But if you think it looks too cold and clinical, reduce the amount by having the sink bowl let into the work-top (make it bowls if you're stingy with your washing-up water (*14.2); then you can have one full of clean rinsing water). And either way, if you have a dishwasher (*14.3), think twice before you allocate precious draining space to it, because you're still going to have to wash and drain the extra-dirty dishes and pans that the dishwasher jibs at. Better to install it immediately beyond the sink or, if your back's in good shape, somewhere beneath it.

If you live in a flat, or hate trekking out to the dustbin on wet nights, have your sink fitted with a waste disposal unit (*14.4). This will eat up practically everything apart from tins, bones, paper cartons and bits of string that get wrapped round the works. And don't think you *have* to have your sink unit positioned under the window. It's true that because of the cost of laying drainage pipes, sinks have to be installed against or at right angles to an outside wall. But if you spend longer preparing meals than washing them up (and most people do) why not have the preparation area under the window, so you can keep an eye on the children in the garden or simply enjoy the view? Meantime, wherever you put your sink, remember to store saucepans and casseroles nearby, because nine times out of ten you're going to need water before you can start cooking. Another point to remember is that the farther away you put a plumbed-in washing machine (and it *should* be plumbed in—trailing flex and hose pipes are unwieldy and dangerous) the higher the plumbing costs.

Finding room for a freezer

Most people can find room for a fridge in a kitchen, but freezers (*14.5) are a different matter, because the more you get the hang of freezing the bigger you want your freezer to be. If you're short of floor-space rather than wall-space, you may be able to solve the problem with a fridge-freezer—say one with a 7 cu. ft freezer below a 7 cu. ft fridge. But if you're short of both, rather than buy a small one that doesn't begin to cope with your needs, buy a big one and site it anywhere that's reasonably cool and dry. Inside the house, consider under the stairs, on the landing, in the attic, basement or spare bedroom. Outside the house, consider the garage or even garden shed. All you have to do is organise a 13 or 15 amp. socket for plugging it into. And if you're feeling affluent, why not squeeze a small freezer into the kitchen somehow (HOOVER make a mini-version that can perch on top of the fridge) and keep it stocked from a big freezer that lives elsewhere?

KITCHEN PLANNING DO'S AND DON'TS

Just to recap and include a few more details, here's a list of do's and don'ts. They're a counsel of perfection, but you'll probably be able to adapt them to what's physically and economically feasible for you.

Things you should do

1 Plan a good work sequence with four main areas: for food preparation, cooking, serving and washing up.

2 Use storage logically. Crockery and cutlery should be near the eating or serving area; kitchen tools and dry stores like flour and sugar near the preparation area; cooking tools, spices and seasonings near the cooker. Store things you rarely use in the awkward-to-reach areas; in top cupboards, at the bottom of base units or in corner units.

3 Set wiring into the wall and have plenty of electric points installed at counter height, to save unnecessary bending. You could need at least ten universal 13 amp. socket outlets, one 30 amp. cooker outlet (two for split-level cooking), a 20 amp. water heater outlet if necessary, and a 13 amp. outlet for the waste disposal unit.

4 Plumb in dishwashers and automatic washing machines. Even if you can't afford them to begin with, have the plumbing and wiring done in readiness and leave a space for them under the work-tops. Then you can fill the gaps with open shelving until you're ready to buy them.

5 Check with your local authority before installing a waste disposal unit; not all drainage systems can cope with them. And if you can't afford one yet but want one later, make sure your sink has the right-sized waste-hole ($3\frac{1}{2}$ in.) to accommodate one.

6 Provide adequate ventilation. Cooker hoods are much more efficient than window extractors, which are very good at extracting heat from kitchens on cold winter days. There are two types: ducted hoods, which whizz cooking smells on their way to the outside world by means of a duct, and re-circulating hoods (ideal for internal kitchens) which kill off smells within the kitchen.

7 Have one slightly lower working surface for jobs such as rolling pastry—possibly a table if you've room for one.

8 Buy units with adaptable work heights, because the BSI-recommended 900 mm (36 in.) may be too high for you. Many units can be varied a few inches by plinths or the thickness of the work surface. If a few inches isn't enough, buy a wall-hung system like CONRAN's, and fix it as low or high as you like.

9 If you're short of space (remember you need 42 in. between units if cupboard doors aren't to crash in mid-air) buy units with sliding doors by firms such as KANDYA, CONRAN and THOMAS EASTHAM.

10 Look for hidden extras that may make your life easier. Like HYGENA 2000's pull-out ironing board, and 'built-in' hotplate trolley that can be wheeled into the dining room. Or the recent ELECTROLUX range of units, where doors lift off for easy cleaning and shelf positions can be varied.

11 Organise efficient lighting. Fluorescent lighting is best because it throws shadow-free light that's ideal for working. If you hate the look of it, have it discreetly fixed to the near underside of your wall cupboards where it can light the work surfaces directly and unobtrusively. Then you can have something attractive—perhaps a converted-to-electricity oil lamp—hanging from the ceiling for general lighting. Be cautious with spot-lights. They're efficient, good-looking, and capable of being angled to throw light just where you want it. But they give off a lot of heat and can have you wilting on a hot summer's day.

Things to avoid
1 Buying any units till you know what's available. Send off for everyone's brochures (*14.6) and compare quality and prices.

2 Putting the cooker, oven or hob near the door; it's asking for accidents.

3 Forgetting which way unit, fridge and cooker doors hinge. You've usually got a choice, so there's no excuse for mid-air collisions, or doors that can't

Even if you live in a modern town house, you could easily create an old-fashioned 'country' kitchen like this one. Here, do-it-yourself kitchen units in tongued-and-grooved pine look suitably rustic, as do the traditional quarry tiles on the floor. Optional country extras: the big wooden table, the stripped pine chairs, and the exposed brickwork.

be opened fully because they're up against a wall.

4 Forgetting that a door opening into the kitchen wastes about 7 sq. ft of floor space. If you can't afford it, use a bi-fold door, a sliding door or a split-down-the-middle swing door so you can hold dishes with both hands and nudge your way through with your shoulders.

5 Having work surfaces less than 900 mm (36 in.) long (or wide if your haven't caught up with BSI usage yet). Otherwise there won't be enough elbow room to do a job properly.

6 Storing heavy items at the top of wall cupboards; lifting them down will be a risky enterprise.

7 Muddling the laundry section together with the cooking. If you've got a

Sale, Stone & Senior

Genuinely country kitchen boasts bang-up-to-date equipment that doesn't look in the least out of place. Units and cooker stick to white so they merge unobtrusively with the white-painted brickwork; the AGA cooker also comes in a range of vibrant colours.

larder going free, and it doesn't create too many plumbing problems, why not quarry-tile the floor and turn it into a laundry 'room'?

8 Building in boilers etc. so thoroughly that the kitchen has to be torn apart if they need servicing or mending.

9 Buying gadgets unless you're going to benefit from them. It's a sad fact of life that some of the best-equipped kitchens are some of the least-used.

10 Inviting accidents if you've got young children. Ideally, the kitchen should have a play area separated from the rest by a peninsular unit and firmly shut stable door. Look for cookers or hobs with the control panel up alongside the rings, instead of on the front where they can easily be twiddled. Or even more ideally, buy two 2-ring hobs and position them in a line against the wall, so that exposed elements and saucepans are out of children's reach.

11 Hanging curtains near the cooker where they might go up in flames. Go for Venetian blinds, or pretty and practical roller blinds that can be wiped clean.

CREATING A MOOD
Some people feel more efficient in a kitchen that looks like a hospital surgery. Others feel more creative in a comfortable kitchen that has plenty of character. Obviously the basic equipment stays streamlined and modern in both cases (*14.7) but there's tremendous scope for creating mood when it comes to what to put on the floor and walls.

Deciding on the floor
It goes without saying that *whatever* you put on the floor should be practical, hard-wearing and easy-to-clean. Most people plump for vinyl sheeting or tiles which just need mopping clean—though if there's a door opening straight on to the garden, it's worth adding a small non-slip mat just inside so that grit doesn't get tramped in to scratch the surface. But if vinyl's stuck to a concrete sub-floor (it should be especially well-stuck round the sink and washing machine, incidentally, so water-spills don't warp and lift it) it can feel cold and hard underfoot. In this case, consider spending a little extra for 'cushioned' vinyl that feels soft and springy, or vinyl with a felt back for extra warmth and insulation. And don't think vinyl has to look cold and Spartan. In deep, plain colours it can look rich and inviting—though it *will* show every breadcrumb. And if you're after a 'beaker full of the warm south' (and aren't too much of a purist) AMTICO makes a Provençal tile patterned vinyl that doesn't give itself away until you drop a plate and it bounces.

   Quarry or ceramic tiles: Of course, plates *won't* bounce if you decide on a quarry tile floor (guaranteed to make any town kitchen look as if it lives in the country) or a ceramic tile floor (that can have your kitchen looking as sunny and extrovert as a Mario and Franco restaurant). These are both extremely practical and good-looking, though hard on the feet.

Cork and linoleum: If you're not prepared to sacrifice comfort for appearance, then vinyl-faced cork tiles offer a way of having your cake and eating it. They're warm in feel and texture, can be damp-mopped clean and if you choose the tawny natural colour, they'll do a good job disguising muck and crumbs until you're ready to give them a clean sweep. The only snag is that they can be slippery; a criticism that's sometimes levelled at linoleum floors (less practical than vinyl, but very handsome in plain, rich colours).

Carpet: If you're a real sybarite and feel you need spoiling, the ultimate in comfort is kitchen carpets. These are made of nylon or acrylic fibres, so spills don't soak in immediately. In theory, you're supposed to stop what you're doing and mop up the damage before it has time to soak in, but if you don't fancy dropping everything in the middle of making a sauce, you'll probably be better off with carpet tiles, made from a tough hair and synthetic fibre mixture. Then when a tile gets hopelessly stained and sodden, you can lift it out for a vigorous scrubbing at the sink, or if it's past recovery, replace it with a new one.

Natural rush matting: This *isn't* recommended for kitchens (it's slippery, easy to trip over and there's a limit to how much you can scrub it) but even the dourest kitchen expert has to admit it lends kitchens a warm and friendly charm. So do sanded and sealed floorboards; but the charm wears thin once you've spent hours digging spilt food out of the cracks.

Wall surfaces for the kitchen

Like floors, walls need to be tough and practical to cope with condensation and splashes. Scrubable vinyl wall coverings are very attractive when they're plain and agreeably textured though not so attractive when they're patterned with phoney red peppers and bottles of Chianti. Washable wallpapers are reasonably practical (COLES do some very good-looking Portuguese tile patterns) but they're not really up to being put behind the cooker and sink where they'll get marked by fat and water splashes. Here you're better off with gloss paint (provided your walls are even and you don't suffer from a condensation problem) or some form of wall tile (*14.8), whether you choose intricately patterned ceramics or dead-plain stainless steel. These *are* expensive, but sometimes it costs less to cover the whole kitchen with them than you'd think, because once you subtract the areas taken up by windows, doors, base units and wall cupboards, there isn't much exposed wall left. And even if there is, you can always use cheap plain tiles and give them a lift with a scattering of craftsman-made patterned ones.

Shiny ceramic wall tiles *can* look cold if they're teamed with equally shiny vinyl floors, icy stainless steel, and acres of gleaming plastic laminate. If your kitchen's in bad need of humanisation, clad the walls with tongued and grooved pine, sealed and left natural so you can follow the grain of the wood; or if you think that's become too much of a cliché, stained and sealed in a vibrant colour or simply painted white. Either way, it'll add the character that all natural materials bring and make your kitchen a welcoming place to work in.

How to humanise a kitchen

As far as unit manufacturers are concerned, the wheel's beginning to come full circle. The bleak, antiseptic look is on the way out and colour is zinging back into the kitchen with brilliant laminates—even pink candy-striped kitchens for people who like their kitchens pretty. What's more, wood is experiencing a revival—*real* wood, not fake laminate wood grains that never were convincing. Some manufacturers (like GREENCRAFT with their pine units, and MULTIFLEX with their oak or sapele mahogany units) leave the wood natural for a simple, country impact. Others, like BEEKAY-BAUKNECHT, stain the wood to bright, vibrant colours. And though these are fairly upmarket examples, it's perfectly possible to buy cheaper whitewood units by firms like LIDEN, sand and seal them to a honeyed glow, and add small brass or white china knobs for simplicity.

Wood, like all natural materials, introduces a warmth and friendliness of texture that's easy to live and work with. Even small quantities of 'living' things work wonders; perhaps a wooden chopping block, a wicker bowl full of vegetables, wooden spoons in a pottery jar or a plant in a pot. Kitchen decoration isn't something that has to be added artificially. It can arise naturally from well-chosen, functional objects (*14.9). This is why, to the embarrassment of Homes Editors, the 'before' pictures of kitchens always look better than the 'after' ones in magazine features. The 'before' picture is taken when the kitchen has been done on a shoestring, and has open pine shelving full of old oval dishes from junk shops, chunky pottery casseroles and colourful mugs hanging from hooks. The 'after' is taken once our up-and-coming young executive has arrived and everything's expensively hidden behind wall cupboards.

Perfection is something that can be all-too-perfect. In fact, the perfect kitchen is one that works for you—and only *you* can decide what that is.

15 AND SO TO BED

Avant-garde architects have been telling us the bedroom is obsolete for so long now, it's nearly as boring as being told that we spend a third of our lives in bed. What horrifies them is the thought of a room lying idle for most of its working life. They want it used round the clock as a bedsitter or study-bedroom—and of course, if anyone's desperate for space, the idea's perfectly sensible.

But what architects overlook is the fact that most of us dull, conservative

Run-of-the-mill bedroom in a town house gets lifted right out of the ordinary, not with limitless funds but with a brilliant confidence trick. Look closely at the 'four-poster' and you'll see what we mean. The posts are there, but the 'canopy' is simply a block of colour, painted in two shades of orange across the ceiling and down the wall. Formal arrangement of oil painting, lamps and mahogany chairs dares anyone to see through the device.

John Bethel

lot actually *like* conventional bedrooms. There's nothing to equal the relief of shutting the door on unmade beds and trails of clothing when we're in a hurry. Of having somewhere private and quiet to retreat to when the day gets too much to bear. Of being able to leave the evening's stale cigarette smoke in the living room and sleep in a 'new' room that's full of fresh air.

Saying goodbye to the bedroom suite

Whether architects like it or not, the bedroom's here to stay—even if it has got smaller and smaller, so that today's 'master' bedroom is little bigger than yesterday's boxroom. This contraction explains why the cumbersome trio of wardrobe, dressing table and chest of drawers (once seen as an indissoluble part of the marriage vows) has practically vanished from the scene. Unless getting into bed's to be a nightly obstacle race, there just isn't room in the average bedroom for isolated pieces of furniture any more. This is why built-in bedroom furniture has been accepted so readily. Because it can extend from floor to ceiling, it stores much more than the traditional bedroom suite ever could. And because it can extend from wall to wall, confining everything to one, unobtrusive run, it frees at least 25 per cent more floor area. All of which makes the room look much larger—and also makes whizzing over the carpet with a vacuum cleaner a pleasure, instead of an irritating manoeuvre through a forest of furniture.

Incidentally, even reservations about the 'bleakness' of unit furniture can easily be dispelled. All-white Melamine-surfaced units *do* look cool and aloof (that's their appeal, along with practicality) but if you want something friendlier, buy units where the wood's left natural. Or paint them a warm colour. Or paper them to match the walls, using beading to prevent the wallpaper peeling, as we show on page 60. Or cover them with fabric to match your curtains—consider paper-backed hessian if your bedroom needs the interest of texture.

Choosing bedroom storage

Metrication doesn't seem to have done anything to simplify the muddle of measurements bedroom storage comes in. Some firms like HEAL's, and MEREDEW with their *Crystal* range, keep to a strict modular system that measures 2,250 mm high (7 ft 6 in.), 575 mm and 1,150 mm long (1 ft 11 in. and 3 ft 9¾ in.), and 600 mm (24 in.) wide—what we'd formerly have termed deep. As we've already seen in Chapter 9, since the length of each part is an exact multiple of 100 mm (4 in.), it's possible to fit any wall without leaving more than a 50 mm gap (2 in.) at each end; quite an advantage over systems that come in, say, 22 in. long parts, that would leave an 8 in. gap on a 7 ft wall.

Obviously it's best to buy a modular system, if only because in the not-too-distant future, all manufacturers *should* be using the 100 mm module. But it's not so critical as when you're buying kitchen units, because bedroom storage comes complete; unless you're trying to integrate a metric-sized bed (*15.1) within a storage alcove, you don't have to worry about whether another manufacturer's products will fit in.

The main thing to watch for is the width (what we used to call depth) of the wardrobe units. Unless this is at least 600 mm (24 in.), heavy clothes on hangers are going to rub at the front and back, and get worn by the friction before you even get as far as putting them on. Most systems only offer one arbitrary width, but if you're trying to span a wall with a chimney breast and alcoves, keep hunting for manufacturers who make narrower units specially to cope with the situation. Height and length of units is less important—they can easily be made to fit: upwards with top cupboards and/or a scribing piece; sideways with a dressing table shelf filling an awkward gap and/or scribing pieces at either end. Obviously space behind scribing pieces can't be *used* at all (they're only there to give a look of built-in perfection) but top cupboards can be very useful for things you don't need to get at often, such as suitcases and spare blankets and pillows.

It seems ridiculous to attempt 'rules' for bedroom storage when everybody's needs are different. One research organisation's (*15.2) study estimated that the 'average' woman needs 42 in. of hanging rail in a wardrobe; the 'average' man only 24 in. Both allowances seem pretty meagre (especially when you need to allow 3 in. between each hanger to prevent clothes getting crushed) but heaven help any male who prefers hanging up his clean shirts to folding them away in drawers; on 'average', he'd hardly have room left for a single suit.

The best approach is to accept that clothes expand to meet the space allotted to them and aim for as much hanging space as possible. And if you have to make do with a little, don't waste the space below short clothes like suits, skirts and blouses. Arrange a two-tier rail system, so you can hang them one below the other, leaving just a small single-rail section for long clothes like coats and evening dresses.

Cutting down on the frills

In the days of kidney-shaped dressing tables with frills round the base, most people took it for granted that bedrooms were meant to be fussy and 'feminine' places. They tarted them up to the nines with knickerbocker drapes at the windows, floral-patterned carpet on the floor and enough flounces round the bed to rival a tutu. The minority who turned their backs on such sinful frivolity distempered the walls, put freezing cold lino on the floor and slept in surroundings as Spartan as a cell.

Nowadays we seem to have found a happy medium, perhaps partly because unit furniture demands more simplicity and perhaps partly because the 'little woman' mentality is dying out. At any rate, today bedrooms are generally warm, welcoming *and* self-respecting.

Much of the warmth comes from fitted carpet. Because bedrooms don't get much wear and tear, this is one area where cheap carpet won't prove a false economy. And because feet have wiped themselves clean walking up the stairs, you can pick a plain, light colour—off-white if that's your idea of ultimate luxury. Certainly it seems a shame to pick a patterned carpet in

Sophisticated setting for a teenage girl proves bedrooms can be feminine without being fussy. Furniture keeps to cool white; vinyl floor comes in a subtle putty—and was preferred to carpet instead of tolerated as a second best. Curtains at window and round bed provide pattern in a restrained way—and even the four-poster, usually an excuse for frills and flamboyance, maintains a clean-cut simplicity.

the one room where you can afford not to, especially when plain ones 'stretch' a limited floor space to look much larger than it really is. There's no danger of the room looking dull, even when the bedroom storage is so discreet that it hardly gets noticed. Because every bedroom has a natural focal point—believe it or not—the bed (*15.3).

Giving the bed importance
Ideally, the bed should be placed sideways on to the window (place it under

or between window and door, and draughts will be whistling past your ears all night). But wherever you put it (*15.4) it's going to be the first thing you see when you walk in the room. So make sure it's worth looking at.

The simplest way is to give it a really attractive bedspread (*15.5) in place of that tired old candlewick that's been nearly beaten to death in the washing machine. It could be an old-fashioned patchwork that's ablaze with hexagonal pattern and colour. It could be a Spanish tapestry bedspread that's scattered with flowers and thickly fringed. Or it could be a perfectly plain bedspread that's piled high with brilliant-coloured cushions for instant impact.

Alternative to a headboard: Unless headboards (*15.6) are intrinsically pretty, forget them. They don't serve a useful purpose, and they're usually a hideous visual distraction. If you want a more formal effect, make a fitted bedspread with inverted pleats at the corners, and carry the fabric up the wall behind to form a matching panel that's exactly the same width as the bed. This works particularly well in a bed alcove—and if you haven't got one, it's easy to make. Simply arrange your wardrobe units so there's a bed-width gap between them and carry top cupboards over the gap. Then you can cover what's left of the wall with the fabric and push the bedhead right up against it, or fix a narrow bed-height shelf between the wardrobe units first. This way when the bedhead butts up against the shelf, the shelf can act as a bedside table to take lights, books, alarm clock and so on.

If you want a more dramatic mood, make a canopy that'll give your bed all the flamboyance of an eastern potentate's. Fix a corona (*6.3) to the ceiling, so that fabric can flow from it in generous folds, and drape to both sides of the bed. This is a treatment that takes nerve—and a fairly high ceiling, if the result isn't to look merely ridiculous.

Make a four-poster: If your room's large enough to take it and you're a romantic at heart, consider a four-poster. This needn't be expensive. All it needs is a frame (incorporating a curtain track) fitted to the ceiling, and four uprights (humble dowelling will do) for tying the curtains back to. Curtain fabric should match or relate to the bedspread of course, and the effect will be much grander if you add a scalloped, castellated or swagged pelmet to the frame.

Shelving the problem: If you prefer things dead simple, play up the basic rectangle shape of your bed by giving it a no-nonsense duvet with a plain but bright-coloured cover. Then integrate the bed within its surroundings by running a shelf at mattress level all along the bed wall. Finally, paint the shelf to match the duvet cover—and not only will it provide the eye with an unbroken line of colour but you'll be able to use the shelf as bedside tables too.

Making the bed disappear

A bed makes a logical focal point in a bedroom, but in a bedsitter that's trying its best to look like a living room the last thing you want it to do is dominate. The neatest way of 'losing' a bed is to buy one that folds up into the wall—preferably into a part of a run of storage so you can close cupboard doors on it. STAPLES make 6 ft 3 in. long beds in 2 ft 6 in., 3 ft or 4 ft widths that can be folded away with bedclothes intact. This point is worth serious consideration because it's no fun having to make a bed when you're so tired all you want to do is fall into it.

The daybed-settee: Bear it in mind if you're looking for a sofa-bed. Very few of them allow the 'bed' to be folded back into the 'sofa' with bedclothes intact, and what's worse, very few of them offer either a comfortable sofa or a comfortable bed. Perhaps it's better to accept that upholstery won't be soft and luxurious and go for something much cheaper, like HABITAT's daybed-settee. Here the seat or mattress is made of 4 in. thick foam, resting on wooden (and very good for the back) slats. The back cushions simply get jettisoned at night, and though you're still faced with the bed-making chore, at least you haven't paid through the nose for the privilege. (If you use sheets and a duvet, you can be in bed in a couple of minutes; if you use an ordinary sleeping bag, you can be in bed in a couple of seconds.)

Creating an illusion: What if you've already got a conventional single bed? Push it lengthways against the wall and back it with cushions so it looks like a sofa. The most effective way is to make a tailored bedspread with inverted pleats that'll fit over your bedclothes (minus the lump of the pillows, of course; they can live in the wardrobe during the day). Then cover square or rectangular cushions with the same fabric, add fabric loops and hang them from a brass pole fixed to the wall about 18 in. above the bed.

It's not an ideal arrangement, especially as you have to make the bed before you go to work in the mornings or come back to a state of chaos. There's nothing like the luxury of a bedroom you can shut the door on—but that's where we came in. . . .

16 GREAT TO GROW UP IN

The ideal nursery is one that grows up with your children. This seems a little hard in the first flush of parenthood, particularly if you're longing for pretty pastels and bunny-rabbits with everything. But the sad fact is that babies don't notice them (they're far more interested in leaves brushing against the window-pane) and toddlers soon start thinking them babyish. The best approach is to keep things simple—go for whatever's practical and adaptable—and worry about the pretty extras after.

The nursery floor

Once again, it's wisest to start with the flooring. What you need is something quiet, so you can tip-toe in late at night to see all is well; something easy-to-clean, so you can wipe up spilled orange juice (and worse!); something hard-wearing, because in no time at all that soft, pliant bundle is going to be charging in with half the local cowboys and Indians.

This rules out most carpets, though you could try non-absorbent and hard-wearing nylon carpet, preferably with a rubber backing. At all events avoid a long-pile carpet, not just because it's impractical, but because it will stop toy trains and cars dead in their tracks. For older children, carpet tiles make sense too, because you can replace individual tiles as they get stained or worn out—but they're far too scratchy for tender knees at the crawling stage and so is handsome and hard-wearing sisal. Sheet lino, vinyl or vinyl tiles are all tough and easy to clean and they needn't look cold and soulless, if you introduce plenty of warm colours elsewhere (if you do have a rug it must be heavy or fixed so it can't slip and cause an accident). But the really ideal flooring is cork. This comes in easy-to-lay tile form, and if you buy it ready-sealed (which deepens the natural colour to a friendly honey tone), you can simply mop spills off the surface. It isn't cheap, but it's soft, warm and quiet to walk on, very hard-wearing and so good-looking that even the most fastidious teenager will have to admit he still likes it.

Antidotes to jammy handprints

Walls are your next problem. Life's going to be a constant battle against sticky fingermarks and scribbles, so try to forestall them from the outset. First,

Graham Henderson

1 Bright and fun-loving nursery has an eye to the future. Filled with brilliant-coloured kids' things now (that's a kite looping across the ceiling), all it needs is a few years, and the felt-covered chimney breast will be covered with pin-ups instead of school paintings; the shelves full of hi-fi equipment instead of treasured collections; and the big pull-out boxes under the laminate worktop full of files instead of toys. As brown sisal carpet will still be going strong, it will only take a few vibrant objects to create a fresh colour scheme in the still non-colour surroundings. **2** Bright-as-a-marigold nursery is practical enough to withstand the toughest tomboys around. White vinyl tiles on the floor are practically indestructible; 'fairground' roller blind is vinyl-finished, so grubby fingermarks can be wiped off; and furniture and woodwork are painted in a tough Polyurethane paint to withstand scuffs. True the walls are painted in impractical emulsion—but that's on the basis that it's easy to slap on a fresh coat and have it dry in a morning. Worth noting: each bunk bed has its own light (top one wall-fixed and out of picture), so there are no quarrels about who puts out the light.

provide a scribbling area. There's no guarantee your child will stick to it, but at least it'll cut down the ravages elsewhere. This can be a blackboard screwed to the wall, or better still, part of a wall or door painted with blackboard paint. In fact, there's no reason why you shouldn't paint all the walls with blackboard paint up to a height of 3 ft 6 in. provided you top it with a brilliantly-coloured frieze for light relief.

Next, be realistic about what you put on the walls. If you're determined to have a nursery-patterned wallpaper, buy a cheap one. It *will* show every jammy hand print (this is true even if it's washable, because washable wallpapers can only take gentle washing, and gentle washing won't get off encrusted raspberry jam), but by the time it's looking thoroughly disreputable, your 'baby' will be criticising the pattern anyway. This is much better then buying an expensive vinyl wall covering with a pattern of ballerinas or spaceships that gets outgrown long before it's outworn. Of course, *plain* vinyl wall coverings *are* the perfect answer for nurseries. They're scrubable (literally) and if, for instance, you buy an agreeably tweedy-textured one, it might even see your toddler through to teenage stage without any complaints.

If you prefer to paint the walls, gloss shrugs off fingermarks easily, but looks cold and clinical; it also accentuates any unevenness in the surface. Eggshell paint is a sensible compromise; hard enough to wash, but matt enough to look fairly friendly. And although emulsion paint is obviously impractical (you *can* wash it, but it soon goes bald in patches) it's so easy to apply that many people just accept they're going to have to splosh round with the paintbrush every few months and do it with good grace.

Don't put out the light

Lighting, of course, has to grow up too. In the early years, most children like some kind of night-light to convince them the Daleks aren't coming. This can be a special low-powered light bulb (enough for a reassuring glow but not enough to keep anyone awake) or simply a light left burning on the landing with the nursery door left ajar. In fact as even a 100-watt bulb burning for 10 hours costs rather less than 1p to run, according to the Electricity Council, why not get used to this luxury? Then children and adults can find their way to the lavatory without stumbling into walls, groping for door knobs, and practically bursting before they collapse gratefully on the seat. 'Saving electricity', incidentally, can turn out to be a false economy; with fluorescent as opposed to tungsten lights, you can cost yourself more than you save, if you keep switching them on and off frequently.

As children graduate to hobbies and homework, be sure to add local lighting above any desk or work top; also a good light above or around a teenage girl's mirror—otherwise she'll only start using yours. And if your children are stacked upwards in bunk beds, give them a wall-fixed light each. This will create reasonably private pools of light (a bottom-bunk occupant should be able to sleep without the avid reader in the top bunk disturbing him) and it'll end the 'last one into bed switches off the light' race, that often ends up in a draw followed by a lengthy dispute.

Splashes of colour: Once you've got the shell of your 'timeless' nursery, it's easy to add inexpensive extras that can be changed later. Young children love bright colours, so give them an orange roller blind, for example, and stick vibrant-coloured friezes round the walls. Paint furniture a bright yellow (you can always paint it white in the future). Fix a piece of pegboard over a desk, so children can hang their treasures from it and paint it a brilliant colour too. All these splashes of colour, plus the usual muddle of toys on the floor and paintings on the wall, will provide enough interest to keep any child happy.

Furnishing for the future

Children grow up so fast they outgrow furniture (* 16.1) nearly as quickly as clothes. This doesn't matter if you want a large family—you can pass furniture down and keep it in continual use. But as most of us seem to be sticking at 2.4 children, it makes sense to choose items that will grow up with them.

It *is* difficult to resist a prettily be-ribboned bassinet with a first baby, but it'll be redundant within three months. Much better to tuck him up in a 'Moses' wicker basket (* 16.2), lined against draughts in a pretty towelling, gingham or other cotton fabric. Buy one with a matching stand to save possible backache and make sure the wheels won't skid or slide on a lino or vinyl floor. A Moses basket can also go on the back seat of the car, though for transporting your baby about you'll probably find a carry cot more convenient. Carry cots aren't advisable for times when you're not going to be able to keep an eye on him, though they're useful when he accompanies you out to dinner as well as for general travel. When buying one avoid a lining of soft plastic that your baby might not be able to breathe against and check as before that the stand is stable and non-skid. Look for the Kite Mark and British Standards Institution number 3881—and don't consider buying one without it.

The second stage: The next essential is a cot. Here you can either buy one that's simply a cot, dismantle it when it's outgrown and store it till it's needed again, or buy a cot that converts into a bed. There's one on the market, with a dropside and solid foot and headboards. The foam-filled and washable 4 ft-long mattress has two 2 ft sections of mattress below, so that when it's too small, all you have to do is remove the sides, pull out the base, fill in the gaps with the extra bits of mattress and you've got a 6 ft-long divan. Whatever type of cot you buy, again, look for the Kite Mark and either BS 1753 or BS 3089. This will ensure a safe dropside; the use of non-toxic paint (most babies like a good gnaw while they're teething); a safe distance between the bars (less than 3 in. so tiny heads can't get stuck); sufficient inside height (at least 23½ in. to discourage climbing); and no more than 33 in. from the dropside when dropped to the floor (despite sophisticated fastening devices, intelligent one-year-olds sometimes manage' to drop the side down and then drop themselves down).

Tiers without tears

How soon is a 'baby' ready for a bed? As soon as he finds his cot bars a challenge and starts clambering over them. Now that beds have gone metric, the small single bed size is 2 ft 11½ in. by 6 ft 2¾ in. (90 cm by 190 cm)—just as well, because children travel around in their beds a lot more than adults, and 2 ft 6 in. wide beds were never really big enough for them. The new size is ideal if you've only got one child in your nursery. But many people have at least two—and that's why the bunk bed business is booming. These show surprising ingenuity of design. You can get bunk beds that split into single beds (useful if you're hoping to move to a larger home some day); bunk beds with storage drawers below, even bunk beds with a spare divan underneath. As there isn't a British Standards specification, check for yourself that the top bunk's safety rail really is safe and that the ladder's sturdy and easy to climb.

All kids love bunk beds (a bit too much—there's usually a fight for the top) but mums are likely to hate them unless they forget conventional forms of bedding. It's no fun trying to tuck in sheets and blankets when you're stuck halfway up a ladder, so why not buy duvets that simply need pulling straight (duvets, by the way, aren't safe to use for babies but as soon as a child is old enough to graduate to a bed, they're ideal). If you're worried about cleaning, some duvets come with a man-made fibre filling and can be machine washed. Or if you prefer, a sleeping bag will do as well.

Stacks of children: The alternative to bunks, of course, is stacking beds — but make sure they can be stacked ready made up. It's bad enough having to make beds in the morning when you're fresh but at night, when you're tired, it's a major operation.

Storage must grow, too

What other furniture do children need in a nursery? Plenty of storage, because although they won't have many clothes when they're young (just wait till they're teenage—they'll have more than you) they'll have masses of toys. There are plenty of mini-wardrobes and chests of drawers in the shops, but they're a gimmicky luxury that'll soon become obsolete. If you want individual items of furniture, it's better to buy full-size versions (although there is a danger here of a wardrobe, say, toppling over if a child climbs inside to play 'houses'). Whitewood is reasonably cheap, and can be painted in bright colours that can be sobered down in later years. But so are old pine pieces that can still be found in junk shops. Because they're old, the odd dents that get banged in them will only add character and they'll look grown-up and sophisticated when the nursery turns into a teenage pad.

Even so, wall-fitted storage, whether built-in or free-standing, provides the most adaptable solution. When interior fittings are flexible (and don't buy any storage system where they're not) you can move up shelves and drawers as the children grow taller. You can also bridge any gap between units with a deep shelf that acts as a desk. This too can go up in the world when the need arises, and in a girl's nursery can quickly turn into a dressing table with a mirror stuck above it.

The only proviso with storage: make sure shelving is fixed firmly to the walls, because toddlers are bound to pull themselves up by it. This goes for anything free-standing too—make absolutely certain there's nothing light enough for them to pull down which is at the same time heavy enough to hurt them. And keep shelving low in the early stages; it's an open invitation to climb, and the higher you fix it the bigger the fall.

Paper furniture: Chairs are about the only items that can't 'grow up'. Fortunately, plenty of people make paper chairs that you can throw away as soon as your children start getting stuck in them. These come in sizzling colours and are tough enough to survive as long as they're needed—some are so cheap you'll probably buy matching tables to go with them. Don't get too carried away though. It's easy to buy so much 'cheap' throwaway furniture that you could have bought a few lasting items in its place.

17 MAKING A SPLASH

Bathrooms used to be bleak, unfriendly places where you whizzed through your ablutions as quickly as you could and emerged covered with virtue and goose pimples. That was when we were a Spartan race. Now we're shamelessly soft—probably a lot cleaner—and our bathrooms are comfortable and luxurious. If yours isn't, here's how to bring about the revolution.

Turning on the heat
Gold-plated taps aren't going to make a bathroom feel luxurious if you're gritting your teeth with the cold. The ideal form of bathroom heating is central heating, but if your system is only partial, or non-existent, an oil-filled electric towel rail takes the nip out of the air and makes soggy towels a thing of the past. These are reasonably cheap—prices start from about £15—but it could cost another £5 to have one fitted. Don't try installing it yourself. There are very strict regulations governing wiring in bathrooms for the simple reason that electricity and water don't mix—if you get between them you could die as a result. That's why heated towel rails have to be permanently fixed and earthed, and why portable electric fires are potential killers. If you want to boost a towel rail's heat, choose a ceiling-mounted infra-red heater with a pull cord, so you don't have to feel for a switch with wet fingers.

Lying back and soaking
If you've inherited a verdigris-stained pock-marked bath (the kind you can't slip into without grazing your bottom) don't put up with it a minute longer. And don't waste time on one of the do-it-yourself re-surfacing kits. They may be cheap but they're not efficient. Of course professional re-surfacing, by a firm like RENUBATH (*17.1), *is* efficient and guaranteed for a year, but as it costs nearly as much as buying a new bath, all you're really saving is the cost of new plumbing.

It's worth replacing just a bath if your sanitary ware is all-white and doesn't need to be colour-matched. Otherwise, most builders' merchants supply very reasonable 'package deals' (*17.2) of matching bath, basin and WC. But a word of warning before you plump for a coloured bathroom suite: if you do, you're restricting yourself to one, or at most two, colour schemes.

120

Sale, Stone & Senior; setting, Diana Austen

If you choose a coloured bathroom suite, make it look intentional. Here, a green bath and basin get strengthened by endless shades of green in everything from the towels and plants to the lick of paint on the cheap slatted table. Easy ideas to pinch: the shelf filling the gap between bath and wall for a built-in look (you could make it a hinged lid instead for an unobtrusive linen basket); the expensive ceramic-tile look that's really cheap sheet vinyl. On the floor, it was simply loose-laid; in the alcove, it was cut into manageable one-yard squares and stuck with impact adhesive.

and you could get thoroughly bored with them as the years go by. Another word of warning: if you've got grandiose schemes for a sunken tub, have you thought what it's going to be like cleaning it—kneeling on the edge and hanging over, or climbing in and scrubbing all around? Still another word of warning if you've fallen for the terribly pretty glass fibre reinforced resin baths, the kind GODFREY BONSACK make (*17.3), where a patterned fabric is bonded on the surface: like perspex baths (*17.4), these can't be cleaned with abrasive scouring powder and it takes real discipline to wash them gently and *regularly*. And finally, don't think a sophisticated black or tobacco brown bath won't show the dirt. It will. Every speck of dust will show up, and as for tidemarks, the dark background will throw soap scum into lurid and highlighted relief.

Since bathrooms grew smaller, the standard bath size has shrunk to 5 ft 6 in. long. Even allowing for the fact that you have to keep your head above water, this means any six-foot-plus hunk of man in your family is doomed to bathe in a Z-shape, with knees stuck up in the air. If you possibly have room, 6 ft-long baths are available for an extra pound or two. (GODREY BONSACK even make a 6 ft 6 in. diameter *circular* bath—but that's going a bit

121

far). Also readily available, 5 ft-long baths for small bathrooms. Probably the smallest bath that's available is the 4 ft-long, 2 ft 4 in. wide TRIDENT perspex bath. Only 18 in. deep, it's ideal for old people (*17.5) who are too frail to lower themselves into a bath completely.

The latest on loos
Whatever you choose to call them, wcs (as they're sternly known in the trade) have come a long way since the high-level cisterns with long, chain handles to pull. A good few feet downwards, in fact, because nowadays low-level cisterns are becoming the rule rather than the exception. The advantage is visual rather than functional: the low cistern only needs about a foot of exposed pipe to connect it to the lavatory pan and the lavatory 'chain' becomes a neat chrome handle that only needs tweeking. Close-coupled wcs are even neater and more compact. Here, the cistern connects directly to the lavatory pan so that there's *no* exposed pipe showing. But the *most* compact of them all is the cantilevered type. Instead of resting on the floor, it's fixed into the wall so it seems to hang in space and not only looks sophisticated and stream-lined, but can be cleaned underneath in a few seconds. Of course, a cantilevered lavatory is only possible if you can afford room for a false wall to hide the pipes and cistern behind. Visually, sacrificing a little space this way makes a bath-room look bigger and less cluttered, but it's not always practicable.

Traditionally, British lavatories have always been the wash-down type, where flushing water roars through the pan as loudly as a lion. But if you're prepared to spend more money, you can buy the siphonic type which empties the pan *quietly* by a combined flush and suction action. In theory, this is supposed to be a much more efficient method of emptying the pan, but in practice, it sometimes results in blockages. So think twice if you've got a young baby, and need to get rid of masses of disposable nappies.

Bidet and be damned
According to Lawrence Wright in his fascinating book on bathroom history, the bidet was first mentioned in 1710, 'when the Marquis d'Argenson was charmed to be granted audience by Madame de Prie whilst she sat'. The bidet's been good for a giggle ever since, though really it's a very useful localised form of bath for washing your feet every bit as much as your nether regions. Unfortunately, it's doomed to be a luxury in this country. The average British bathroom just doesn't have room for one and even if it did, plumbing costs are very high unless there's a nearby lavatory. This is because (quite ludicrously and illogically), waste from a bidet has to go into the soil pipe instead of being allowed to join the bath or wash basin waste. Nevertheless, several British manufacturers are including bidets in their suites; they come either with taps or with a central spray (the latter more costly to install).

Choosing a wash basin
Basically, there are three types of wash basin. The first comes with brackets, so you screw the brackets to the wall and sit the basin on top. The snag here

is that unless you build a false wall to hid the works, you're going to see the hot, cold and waste pipes going down to the floor. The second (and of course, more expensive) type comes with a pedestal, so you screw the pedestal to the floor and sit the basin on top. Unfortunately, the pedestal only hides the waste pipe completely and the hot and cold pipes are just visible, which can be very irritating visually. The third type is an insert basin, meant to be dropped into a vanitory unit. This is obviously the neatest because you not only hide the pipes, but have somewhere to put the Vim and Harpic as well. You can buy vanitory units ready-made, but they're quite easy to make with a laminated plastic-covered top and cupboard front, preferably extending from wall to wall for an expensive, tailormade look. Either way, make sure some provision's been made for your toes underneath the wash basin. Otherwise, you'll be too far away to even wash your hands comfortably.

Other factors need considering, and it'll save you lots of time in the builders' merchants if you make up your mind before you go shopping. What kind of waste do you want, for instance? The kind with a plug and chain hanging from a difficult-to-clean hole in the basin, or the rather more expensive pop-up type? And where do you want the taps—either side, both at one side, in the middle if you've got mixer taps, or best-looking of all, coming directly out of the wall?

Adding a shower

If you get lazy and lethargic the minute you sink into a warm bath (which is great if you've got an hour to spare, but not if you're catching the 8.30 to work), consider having a shower (*17.6) instead. It only takes a few minutes, it's brisk and invigorating, it uses a quarter the amount of water and it's much cleaner.

The beauty of showers is that they take up so little space; 3 ft by 3 ft of floor area is enough, but allow more if you need plenty of elbow room. And remember that you're going to have to step out of the shower into a private area so you can dry and dress yourself. Even if you can't fit one into your bathroom, depending on plumbing costs and privacy, it might be possible to squeeze one into a cupboard or at the end of a passage. Wherever you site your shower, there must be a 3 ft head of water between the bottom of the cold tank and the shower outlet. Otherwise you'll have to buy a booster pump.

How to get splash-happy: Ideally, a shower should be built into a bathroom recess, with the three sides and a drained floor tiled in ceramic or quarry tiles. This way you can get as splash-happy as you like without doing any damage. But unless the bathroom floor's drained, you have to try to confine the water within the recess and a shower tray. Here, plastic curtains (apart from feeling horribly clammy) aren't very efficient. If you can possibly afford the space and money, it's much better to fit a hinged or sliding glass door.

Ready-made cabinets: If you're not prepared to go to the upheaval of making a proper shower enclosure, the simplest solution is to buy a ready-made shower cabinet. Then all you have to do is get it connected to the water supply and waste. It's up to you whether you choose a shower-rose fixed overhead, at shoulder-height, or adjustable by means of a flexible hose. Most serious showerers prefer overhead roses, but avoid them if you can't bear wearing shower caps and don't want to get your hair wet. And whatever you decide, pay the few pounds extra for a thermostat control. That way you won't have to choose between being scalded or frozen to death (particularly important if it's going to be used by an old person whose reactions will be slower).

Over the bath: Fitting a shower to a bath isn't a very happy compromise.

If you choose a white bathroom suite and stick to a non-colour floor (here it's white vinyl tiles, but it could be natural cork or a neutral synthetic carpet), then all it takes is a change of wallpaper and towels to get a completely new colour scheme. At the moment, this bathroom's green, and the colour-message comes over strongly in the fresh-patterned washable wallpaper. Because the room's too tiny to take crazy attic angles without confusion, it's been carried over the sloping ceiling as well. Also over the skylight (not in picture), in the form of a matching roller blind. PS. on greens. Be sure to include plenty of leafy plants; they're bound to thrive in the steamy heat of bathrooms.

You can't really scrub away with abandon while your feet are teetering in the narrow curve of the bath (we're taking it for granted you've a non-slip mat first). And unless you have a tiled and drained floor, you'll need to fix shower curtains or a glass panel alongside the bath so the whole room doesn't become waterlogged.

Last word on equipment
Buying sanitary ware is a very misleading business because everything comes in bits and pieces—and when you add them all up, they're more expensive than you thought. Buy a lavatory, for instance, and you'll probably find the seat and lid are priced separately. Buy a wash basin, and it may not include obvious basics like the waste and plug. Of course, buy even a package-deal bathroom suite and you'll find taps (*17.7) are not only extra but can be as expensive as the sanitary ware itself.

Decorating the bathroom
Most bathrooms are so small they're the one place you can make a big splash without being extravagant. Take the floor area, for instance. It's probably only 3 or 4 sq. yds, so why not lash out on Spanish or Italian ceramic tiles that'll give it a sunny, Mediterranean mood. Or quarry tiles, if you want a simpler, more rustic look. Or ready-sealed cork tiles if you want a warm, friendly-textured look; these look especially good carried up the side of the bath too. Even a fitted carpet, if you choose a synthetic fibre that doesn't soak up water too readily.

There isn't likely to be much wall area either, so why not buy a really expensive washable wallpaper—it'll only need one roll or at most two. (Incidentally, if you fall in love with an ordinary paper and want to make it more practical and splash-proof, paint on a coat of transparent *Gard* or *Fend* to give it a protective finish). Or clad the walls with sealed, tongued and grooved wood (this is less of a cliché fixed horizontally, and looks good covering the bath panel too). Or for a bathroom that will really make your friends envious, cover the walls with a pvc-treated fabric; it looks terrific, and has a practical wipe-clean finish.

The best paint for bathroom walls, if you want to keep them plain and basic, is something like SILEXINE's *Anticon*. As the name implies, this helps prevent condensation forming. (By the way, did you know that you can buy special lightweight plastic mirrors (*17.8) that don't steam up like ordinary mirrors?). And unless your bathroom's very well ventilated, steer clear of gloss paint; this encourages condensation to form. And however beautiful your bathroom, it will look pretty miserable with moisture running down the walls.

18 FINALLY ON THE HOME FRONT

Now you've done up your home on the inside, don't let yourself down with the outside. It's not just a matter of worrying what the neighbours think (though there's no reason why you shouldn't give them a cheer-up), it's a matter of protecting what's probably your chief financial investment. Houses rapidly start fraying at the edges (so would you if you were out in all winds and weather) and it really can be a case of a stitch in time saving nine.

However hard-up you are, make a real effort to decorate externally once every three years. (Incidentally, if you've bought your home leasehold, this might be a requirement written into the lease.) If you don't, you could find yourself spending more money in the long run: on replacing wooden window frames, if rain's seeped through cracked paint long enough to warp them; on re-decorating inside your home, if rain's penetrated the walls and made damp patches; on eradicating dry or wet rot—which can cost a small fortune— if you ignore the damp patches for too long.

The delights of do-it-yourself

It *is* possible to do-it-yourself, but external decoration's a long job and best done in one grim onslaught, rather than short bursts that allow grime to accumulate between each attack. It also has to be done between spring and autumn (bang goes your summer holiday!) because even if *you* can survive winter sleet and frost, the paint won't be able too. Possible paint for do-it-yourselfers is SILEXINE, which claims to be 20–25 per cent cheaper than comparable brands. But send off for everyone's paint leaflets—they're all free and a lot more colourful than travel brochures. If equipment is short, look in the Yellow Pages of the Telephone Directory for hire service shops—they'll have ladders, brushes, even scaffolding if you're being really ambitious. Also polythene sheeting to cover the paths and patio: most amateurs are a bit splash-happy and it's harder getting paint off where you don't want it than applying it where you do.

Instructing a professional

If you're having the work done professionally, it's best to go to a builder and decorator rather than a decorator pure and simple. This way you can ask them

126

to give the outside of your house a thorough overhaul that'll cover everything from the condition of the roof, chimneys and guttering right down to the front gate. Keep reminding yourself that the main aim of external decorating is to make your home weather-proof; making it look pretty is a pleasant bonus. It's no good slapping on a cover-all coat that's going to recoil in peeling horror within a few months—you have to provide a firm, dry, clean surface for it to adhere to.

Deciding what's necessary: If you're having the walls of the house painted, with luck, all they'll need in the way of preparation is brushing down with a stiff brush and sloshing with water. But if they're brick, there may be some loose mortar that will need brushing out and re-pointing; if they're stucco (a smooth sand and cement finish that looks like plaster) holes and cracks will need filling first; and if the surface has had to be stripped back to the original, all the walls will need sealing before painting proper begins.

As for woodwork, a good job will involve the following: burning off defective paintwork; rubbing down all the paintwork—not just to start with, but between each subsequent coat of paint; knotting any bare wood (this means painting the knots with a clear cellulose, so they don't stain through the paintwork); stopping any holes (DIYs please note—there's an *outdoor* grade *Polyfilla* for this purpose); priming any bare wood; adding one or two coats of undercoat; and finishing off with one coat of topcoat.

You'll need to specify all these things when you ask for an estimate—and ask for at least three—because for some funny reason, builders and decorators tend to put in high quotes when they don't want the work instead of telling you outright. There's no sense paying through the nose for what you could get cheaper elsewhere, especially as your detailed specification should protect you against skimping (* 18.1).

Which type of paint? You'll also need to specify which paints—and that means which type as well as which colours. If you're painting stucco, you can use an exterior quality emulsion, which is reasonably hardy. Obviously gloss is more weatherproof, but if your walls are too uneven to take it or you don't like shiny surfaces, but still want the extra toughness, try something like *Sandtex-Matt* or DULUX *Weathershield*. These paints are heavier than exterior emulsion because they have a protective chemical built into their formulas. And by the way, don't try whitewash; the very name should give you the clue that it'll wash away with every shower of rain. People do use it a lot in the country, but that's because they're prepared to re-whitewash their homes every summer along with the out-houses and cow-sheds. If you want an alternative that's nearly as cheap but more permanent and protective, try *Snowcem*—but remember that once you've used it you can't put an ordinary paint on top without first wire-brushing and painting with a stablising solution. Woodwork, at least, is straightforward. Gloss is the only paint that gives enough protection; though of course, you could strip the wood back to natural provided you protected it with three coats of clear lacquer, and rubbed down well between each coat. This is bound to be a lengthy job, but the result can be very rewarding.

Opposite: 1 Country house in Suffolk with *Jonquil* SANDTEX-MATT on the walls and CARSON'S *Brilliant White* Gloss on door and woodwork. Treatment is simple, but lets architectural features like the lacy gable, oriel bay windows and columned door, speak for themselves.

2 Town house sandwiched between its neighbours gets *Hydrangea* CROWN STRONGHOLD on the wall, more CARSON'S *Brilliant White* Gloss at the windows, and MAGICOTE Gloss in *Regal Blue* on the door. Curtains and window-blind wisely stick to white—there's no room for competition in such a narrow house-front.

Choosing the colours

That's the dull side of external decorating. Choosing the colours is the exciting bit, and this applies even if you're saddled with a dull house. Say you've got a redbrick 1930s 'semi', that looks just like all the other redbrick semis in the road. Paint the bricks white and immediately you've got a light adaptable background instead of a heavy restricting one, so you stand out from your neighbours like a shirt in a detergent ad. Then choose sophisticated colours for the woodwork (the house won't have enough distinction to carry off bright colours without looking vulgar). For instance, paint all the windows— and beamed gable if you've got one—with caramel-coloured gloss. Make a window box in segments, to fit round the ground floor bay. Paint the box and the front door in a chocolate brown and fill the window box to the brim with bright orange marigolds. Finally, stand on the opposite side of the road and see how your curtains look. If they're a mass of conflicting colours and patterns, invest in yards and yards of cream curtain lining, and line the lot so they present a unified face to the world.

Let the details tone: Say you've got a tiny Edwardian terrace house. You *could* have the bricks and stonework cleaned to show up the details round the windows and doors, but this is an expensive process that costs far more than painting everything in sight. As you only have to paint the front of the house, however, and the front will be very narrow, consider a gloss paint despite the fact that it costs about twice as much as exterior emulsion. Then, if your neighbouring houses have stayed grey and gloomy, throw caution to the winds and pick a buttercup yellow. But don't get too carried away. Pick out details in a strong contrast and they'll look fussy in such a tiny area—so restrain yourself, and choose a toning colour for the stone and woodwork round the windows and doors. A soft orange will do the trick without looking garish, and the eye will go straight to the front door if you pick out the panels in warm ivory. Again, make sure your curtains or blinds blend with the scheme, and if in doubt, stick to white or cream. (Of course, if in total doubt—not everyone's got the courage to put on a bold front—paint both walls and woodwork white and you can't go wrong.)

Shades of one colour: If you live on an estate, where houses have been built as alike as peas in a pod, assert your personality with a strong and individual colour scheme. The simplest way is to take the one-colour approach suggested in Chapter 5. Say the top half of the house is covered with clap-board; the bottom half brick, which extends along to form the garage. Run the gamut of blue-greens from turquoise to midnight blue, making sure to pick out window and door frames in white for light relief. Paint the clap-board a sea-green, the brickwork a greeny-turquoise and pick out the front and garage doors in midnight blue. And if possible, stick to white at the windows; white Venetian blinds will look crisp and attractive in this context.

The country cottage: Say you live in a brick and timber country cottage. Old bricks have a mellow beauty of their own and it's sacrilege to cover them up, but if they've already been painted by a previous owner, it's probably in white with the beams picked out in a dark stain. This always looks good—but it could look even better. Why not paint the bricks in a soft, gentle *colour* such as Suffolk pink, duck-egg blue or honeysuckle. Then pick out the beams in white, and if the front and back doors are in good enough condition, strip them back to the natural wood, taking care not to damage the roses round the door.

Decorating the front door

Painting the whole of a house is a mammoth task, but it's the general impression that counts. People aren't going to have time to scrutinise each detail as they walk up the path, so provided you're not *too* slap-dash, the brushwork doesn't have to be impeccable. This isn't true of the front door, however. These few square feet get maximum attention (there's nothing else to look at between ringing the bell and waiting for the door to open) so give it as much loving care as you can possibly spend on it. Make sure all the brushstrokes go in one direction (this is much easier—and quicker in the long run—if you remove the door furniture first). And above all, make sure your door furniture can take the kind of examination it's likely to get.

Showing your metal

Door furniture (*18.2) is the cumbersome trade term for knobs and knockers etc., though when you add up all the bits and pieces it's easy to see why they need it. Also easy to see why so many doors are cluttered up with ironmongery. Because it's not just a knob and a knocker, it's a lock (*18.3)—preferably mortice as well as Yale to discourage burglars—a letter-plate, and possibly numerals and a finger-plate as well. There are two ways of coping with these essentials: either buy the neatest and least obtrusive you can find, and let them perform their functions in a basic, no-nonsense way; or buy the most decorative and play them up, so they become a positive and appealing feature.

Keep it simple: Which you do will probably depend on your door and the character of your house—though it won't necessarily depend on whether the door furniture's modern or traditional. Some of the most basic and functional door furniture is Georgian, which could look good on a modern door. Conversely, some modern door furniture is so tasteful and timeless that it could look good on a Georgian door. Even so, it's pretty safe to say that if you live in a modern house, or one where the original panelled door (*18.4) has been replaced with a faceless flush one, it's a mistake to load it with ornate Georgian or Victorian-style brassware, which would merely look ridiculous. Keep things simple—and the simplest you can get is the impeccably-designed *Modric* range in silver anodised aluminium. If you can afford it (and it *is* more expensive than similar door furniture) buy everything you need from this one range, because the designer's really sweated to make sure everything relates perfectly.

The same advice holds good, of course, whoever's door furniture you buy. Stick to the same range throughout, and you'll be sure of good proportions and a satisfying all-over impact. And if you love your postman, fix the letter-plate midway up the door, so he doesn't have to break his back bending down to one practically at ground level. Or if it's a glazed front door with only a wooden frame, consider a vertical letter-plate (you can buy a very neat, stainless steel one, that's a combined knocker, lock- and letter-plate) for halfway up the right-hand frame.

If you have a grander, panelled door, you can go to town with some of the beautiful brass door furniture that's being made today. (And if you buy it ready-lacquered, you won't have to stand out on the doorstep polishing it every day.) Here, it's a matter of getting the scale right. A big, Georgian urn-shaped knocker is bound to look pompous on the door of a small Victorian or Edwardian house and so will a massive brass letter-plate that's at least a foot wide. Go for something more modest unless you're sure your door can take it. And before you go jettisoning what's on the door already, give it a scratch. With any luck it might be the original door furniture, unrecognisable beneath a century's coats of paint.

What about window boxes and hanging baskets? Well that's another story—and you'll find it in GARDENING, another title in the Good Housekeeping Family Library series.

NOTES TO CHAPTERS

1 A HOME IS WHAT YOU MAKE IT

1 One thing we *do* have to accept, however, is the limitations of the area the house is in. And it's a curious fact of life that people often know more about where they're going to spend a fortnight's holiday ('2 mins. from sea, regular bus service to town, good shopping facilities') than they do about where they're going to spend the next 10 or 20 years or so.

Find out first: The right house or flat in the wrong area can make life a misery. Questions to ask are: is there a regular bus service (particularly to the nearest station if you're a British Rail commuter); where are the nearest shops; what kind of schools does the area have to offer? If you're buying a new house,* the site manager should have a leaflet setting out everything, from the nearest cinema and theatre to the nearest golf course. Otherwise the estate agent you're buying the house through should be able to help. If he can't (or won't), there's nothing for it but to do your own research. Ring the local authority for information on schools, swimming pools, libraries etc.

Off the record: But best of all, latch on to a nearby and garrulous neighbour. She's likely to let slip things that go unnoticed during brief visits: that the party walls between houses are so paper-thin you don't need your own radio; that the floors between flats are so badly-insulated you can hear the people upstairs actually using the loo (and we don't just mean flushing the cistern); that having a communal garage is a good idea, except that you're so near it you'll be woken by car doors banging half the night; that cars whizz down the straight stretch of road, and there's nowhere safe for children to play (on new housing estates, look for winding, landscaped roads that slow down cars, and traffic-free paths where you can walk with a pram); that when the wind's in a certain direction, planes make their run-in directly above you (this can be noisy even when you're 10 miles from the airport); that when the wind's in the wrong quarter you get a whiff of the distant gas-works or tannery; that when the leaves have fallen off the trees, you get a lovely view of the next street's garden sheds.

* If you're going to be first in on a new development, make sure it's not going to be a desolate no-man's-land until everyone's moved in. Ask the site manager whether there'll be a finished road, or whether you'll have to tramp through mud for months? If it's a big estate with its own shops, will they open up for just a handful of families; will the local transport company wait till the estate's full before starting a bus service? Unless the building firm's prepared to subsidise such services until they're commercially viable, pioneers can have a tough and depressing time of it.

2 THE WAY YOU LIVE

Central heating really needs a book to itself, but briefly, here are the pros and cons of the various types. First, a look at the different kinds of fuel.

ADVANTAGES

DISADVANTAGES

Solid fuel

Installation and running costs are relatively cheap.
Heats hot water as well as the house.
Boilers seldom need repairing, and are virtually silent. They'll carry on heating water through a power cut (but not the house; radiators will cool when circulating pump stops).

It isn't as clean as other systems.
You have to stoke the boiler by hand.
The heat takes longer to adjust than with other systems.

Oil

Running costs are cheaper than gas or electricity.
Running costs drop as the installation gets bigger, so it's an economical choice for large houses.
Oil will continue to heat water through a power cut, but circulating pump stops.

Installation costs are high.
Boiler needs regular maintenance.
You need plenty of space for a storage tank within access of the refuelling lorry.

Gas

Gas boilers are compact and cheap to install.
Gas needs no storage space, so it's ideal for small flats and houses.
It will continue to heat water through a power (i.e. electricity) cut, but circulating pump stops.

Running costs are higher than for solid fuel or oil (though taking into account installation costs, it's no more expensive than oil in a small-to-medium house).
If the gas supply gets cut off or the pressure drops, you'll have neither heat nor hot water.

Electricity

Cheapest of all to install.
Clean and efficient.
No boiler needed.
Flexible—you can take the radiators with you if you move house.

Most expensive to run, though it helps to be on a White Meter.
You're at the complete mercy of a power cut.

Different types of heating

Storage heaters (electric): These use cheap off-peak electricity at night, store the heat, and release it gradually through the day. The snag is the lack of flexibility—you can't control the heat precisely; most of the day there's only enough for background warmth and if you go out in the evening, you can't switch it off. (Though the fan-assisted type can be switched on to push out extra warmth when it's needed.) Also, storage heaters are still much bulkier than radiators and not very beautiful to look at.

Underfloor heating (electric): This costs a fortune to install unless you're having a new house built or happen to be re-laying the entire ground floor. As it uses off-peak electricity, running costs are no higher than gas but you have to top up with other forms of heating, especially in the bedrooms of a house, as opposed to a one-floor flat. Again, the output of heat is very difficult to control.

Warm air heating: This is usually gas, but can be electric, oil or solid fuel; it really needs to be installed as a house is being built. A heating unit warms the air, which is then fan-blown along ducts to the various rooms, where it's released through low-level grilles. Electric warm air heating can be as cheap as storage heaters, because it uses off-peak electricity. Advantages: starting from cold, the house can be warm in less than an hour (other systems take anything from 2–4 hours); the air is changed and filtered twice an hour, so it's a very clean system; as with underfloor heating, there are no ugly radiators. Disadvantages: Installation is expensive; you usually need a separate water-heating system; if you've got weak eyes, the constant circulation of air will make them water.

General

If a package deal seems cheap, make sure it includes enough radiators to heat your home to the National Heating Centre's recommendation of 70°F in living room and bathroom; 65°F in hall and on landings; 60°F in bedrooms—all temperatures taken when it's 32°F outside. It's not worth the upheaval for only partial heating.

If you need advice, the best place to get it is at the NATIONAL HEATING CENTRE, 34 Mortimer Street, London W1. Basic information is free, but there's a charge for really detailed advice. Perhaps most important of all, the NHC has a list of registered installers, all of whom are legally obliged to give a 2-year guarantee, which is backed by insurance. True you pay for the insurance in the price—but it protects you against the installer going bankrupt—something that frequently happens.

3 SPACE FROM NOWHERE

1 Outside London the Building Inspector covers all aspects of conversions, large or small. In the London area, his job is divided between specialist officers. Here's a list of the people you might find yourself dealing with: the Planning Officer (from whom you get planning consent); the District Surveyor (who sees you comply with the planning consent and deals with all structural matters): the Borough Engineer (who deals with fire regulations; it is up to the DS to see that you comply with them); the Public Health Inspector (who deals with drainage and who may be part of the BE's department). Improvement Grants could be handled by any of the above officers, so ring your Town Hall to find out. If you intend to break a bye-law and need a 'waiver' entitling you to do so write to: The Architect's Department, Greater London Council, Middlesex House, Vauxhall Bridge Road, London SW1.
2 On many estates, it can be cheaper to buy a three-bedroomed house and add a fourth bedroom than to buy a four-bedroomed house outright. However, with new houses, you will need planning permission to add an extension.
3 If your house is listed as being of historical interest, you'll need additional consent from the Historic Buildings Board, Department of the Environment, Caxton House West, Tothill Street, London SW1. If it's given, you'll have to make the extension match the house, which could turn out very expensive.

Recommended reading

Extending Your House (Consumers' Association, 14 Buckingham Street, London WC2). Price £1.

Building Regulations (HM Stationery Office). Price £1.00. Also obtainable through booksellers and from most reference libraries, but difficult for the layman to interpret. *Development Control Policy Notes* (HM Stationery Office: Department of the Environment and The Welsh Office). Price 9p each. Aims to help householders attempting extensions or alterations. Most useful are: *General Principles, Development in Residential Areas* and *Development in Rural Areas*. Also obtainable from booksellers.

USEFUL ADDRESSES
The Housing Centre Trust
13 Suffolk Street
Pall Mall East
London SW1
A mine of information on conversions and all aspects of property. The bookshop is open to the public, keeps nearly everything currently available on housing, and the staff are helpful and don't mind browsers.

Building and design centres
The Building Centre
26 Store Street
London WC1
You can't buy anything here, but you can see what's available and take away leaflets. Information Desk deals with telephone inquiries: 01-636-5400.

The Design Centre
28 Haymarket
London SW1
Again, you can't buy anything here but you can look up in their Design Index to see the best of what's currently available. Cards show photographs and give details of everything that's been passed by the COID's committee; where space permits, latest index arrivals are put on display.

The Building Information Centre
The College of Building and Commerce
Stoke Road
Shelton
Stoke-on-Trent

The Cambridge Building Centre
16 Trumpington Street
Cambridge

Bristol Building and Design Centre
Colston Avenue
The Centre
Bristol

The Liverpool Building and Design Centre
Hope Street
Liverpool
This holds the full COID Design Index and you can look up products here.

The Building Centre of Ireland
17 Lower Baggot Street
Dublin 2

The Building Centre of Scotland
425–427 Sauchiehall Street
Glasgow

The Scottish Design Centre
St Vincent Square
Glasgow C21

Some professional organisations
The National Federation of Builders' and
    Plumbers' Merchants
52–54 High Holborn
London WC1
Write here for address of your nearest Home Improvement Centre, which will help plan improvements and choose fittings; the amount of help they can give is necessarily limited but it should start you on your way.

The National House Builders' Registration Council
58 Portland Place
London W1
This organisation keeps a register of

135

17,000-odd builders who provide a 10-year structural guarantee, backed by insurance, against major defects (minor ones should get dealt with under the builder's 2-year warranty, which runs concurrently). Using an NHBRC-registered builder also protects you against the firm going bankrupt, so it's well worth writing to this address for a list of registered builders in your area.

The Electrical Contractors' Association
55 Catherine Place
Westminster
London SW1

The Association automatically guarantees all electrical installation work carried out by member-firms against bad workmanship. A list of local members is obtainable from this address.

Damp-proof coursing, woodworm and dry rot services

Rentokil Laboratories
Felcourt
East Grinstead
Sussex

Protim Services
36 Queen Anne's Gate
London SW1

Peter Cox Ltd
11 Water Way
Mitcham
Surrey

The above firms provide a country-wide service. Surveys and estimates are free and work is guaranteed for 20 years. For regional branches, write to head offices.

4 CONVERTING A WHOLE HOUSE

1 Many local authorities pay the grant in stages as the work proceeds. If they won't and you're broke, there's nothing for it but to borrow the money (consoling yourself with the knowledge that at least interest on loans for home improvements is tax-deductable).

If you've already got a mortgage, you may be able to get it increased to cover the cost of the works, particularly if you've already paid off quite a chunk of what you owe the building society. If you own the house outright, and haven't hocked the deeds elsewhere, you should be able to arrange a mortgage through a building society, insurance company or local authority without any difficulty. Mortgage-money is the cheapest money going, and you have plenty of time to pay it back.

The next cheapest is a bridging loan from the bank (preferably a straight overdraft rather than a personal loan, which carries higher rates of interest). Bank loans usually need paying back within a year—but this is no problem if you know you're going to get the grant. The most expensive way of borrowing, because the interest rates are so high, is from a finance house, and here the maximum length of time over which repayments can be made is usually 10 years.

Note : The *Money Which?* Tax-Saving Guides, which come out every March, always give a detailed breakdown of how to borrow money most economically.

2 Although you can't legally call yourself an architect unless your name is on the Register of Architects (big reference libraries should have a copy), there's nothing to stop someone calling himself an 'architectural consultant' or anything similar. This doesn't necessarily mean he's inferior to a *bona fide* architect—simply that he doesn't have the same paper qualifications, and hasn't bound himself to the same code of professional conduct (this bars architects from advertising and prevents them from lowering their fees even if they're desperate for work). In fact if anything, in a *Which?* November 1972 survey called *Professional Advice for Building Work*, non-professional architects came out best of all—*and* they were by far the cheapest.

3 *Money to Modernise Your Home*, a helpful booklet available free from all local authorities, lists the 12-point standard as follows: 'To qualify for discretionary grant a dwelling must, where practicable, after improvement or modernisation:

1) be in a good state of repair and substantially free from damp
2) have each room properly lighted and ventilated
3) have an adequate supply of wholesome water laid on inside the dwelling
4) be provided with efficient and adequate means of supplying hot water for domestic purposes
5) have an internal water closet if practicable; otherwise a readily accessible outside water closet
6) have a fixed bath or shower in the bathroom
7) be provided with a sink or sinks and with suitable arrangement for the disposal of waste water
8) have a proper drainage system
9) be provided in each room with adequate points for gas or electric lighting (where reasonably available)
10) be provided with adequate facilities for heating
11) have satisfactory facilities for storing, preparing and cooking food
12) have proper provision for storing fuel (where required).

4 Local authorities have toughened up considerably over the past few months. Often they want to know what the flats are for before they'll agree to give a grant—and if you say for selling, you probably won't get one. Fair enough really.

At the time of going to press, The Housing Act, 1971, which made provision for a Discretionary Grant of up to £1,500 in certain areas (including the North-East, Wales and Scotland, where development needs encouraging), is under review. As things stand, work qualifying for a £1,500 grant has to be completed by 23rd January 1974. What happens then is anyone's guess—but the worst that can happen is that the £1,500 maximum (which, incidentally, can cover 75 per cent of the building costs instead of the usual 50 per cent) will revert to the £1000 that applies everywhere else in the country.

Recommended reading

To improve architect-client relations, read *Mr Blandings Builds His Dream House* by Eric Hodgins. It's out of print, but your local library should be able to ring round the branches and find a copy. A hilarious blow-by-blow account of an American couple having their dream-home built for them. The moral of the story is international—and you'll enjoy the book anyway.

5 HOW TO LIVE WITH THE COLOURS YOU LIKE

1 In January 1973, the British Standards Institution revised their range of British Standard colours. There are now 88, with 12 pure spectral colours, each varied equally to make several differing shades. Paint manufacturers make some or all of these colours, usually plus some colours of their own—'house' colours that have proved popular over the years, or are introduced as they become fashionable.

This means that in theory, one paint manufacturer's BS colour should be exactly the same as another's, even if it goes under a different name (one man's Sage Green may be another man's Lichen). In practice, however, there may be a very slight difference. Not as much as when you try to match knitting wool, but enough to make it safest to stick to the same brand of paint.

In theory again, the BS colours are for use generally. But in practice, a colour that's easy to achieve in paint may be difficult in fabric or carpets, or *vice versa*. Even so, with any luck, the new range of colours will encourage greater co-ordination in furnishings.

If you want the full range of BS standard colours (worth having, because many paint shops simply show you the charts they happen to have), a folder with the full complement of 88 costs £1.90 from the British Standards Institution, 2 Park Street, London W1. And if you want to send off for all the paint manufacturers' colour charts (far too many to list here), you'll find the addresses in Polymers' *Paint and Colour Year Book*, at most big public reference libraries.

PS on paint: If you drip paint up to your elbows when you work, buy a non-drip (thixotropic) paint like BERGER's *Magicote*. If you leave your brushes to set rock-solid after using oil-bound paints, use HADFIELD's acrylic paint for an eggshell finish or ARTHUR SANDERSON of Hull's *Lightning gloss emulsion* for a shiny gloss finish—then brushes can be washed clean with water instead of turps substitute.

2 If you need the help of an expert, *Good Housekeeping's* Colour Planning Service costs £1.75 per room. Send crossed cheque or postal order to: Good Housekeeping Colour Planning Service, Chestergate House, Vauxhall Bridge Road, London SW1.

3 If you can't find just the right shade of carpet and are prepared to pay for it, HUGH MACKAY LTD, at Roman House, Wood Street, London EC2, make carpets in all of the 88 British Standard colours, to order only. So do YOUGHAL CARPETS, at 8 Giltspur Street, London EC1, and if the order's big enough, they'll also weave carpets to special non-BS colours.

For felt and hessian dyed to match paint colours, *8.5.

6 LOOKING AT WINDOWS

1 For details of curtain tracks, write to the following:

Graber Curtain Rails
Marvin Textiles Ltd
41 Berners Street
London W1

Silent Gliss
Star Lane
Westwood Industrial Estate
Margate, Kent

Harrison of Birmingham
PO Box 233
Bradford Street
Birmingham B12

Swish Products Ltd
Tamworth
Staffs

Kirsch
Kirsch Division
Antiference Ltd
Aylesbury, Bucks

Rufflette Ltd
Mount Street
Salford 3
Lancs

2 Pelmets have become *so* unfashionable they're hard to find ready-made. The solution is to make your own from wood, and stick on fabric to match your curtains, plus perhaps a decorative braid. Or make pelmets from fabric alone, stiffening it with VILENE if it's really lightweight. Advantage of fabric is that you can give your pelmet pinch-pleats, castellated edges, or even scalloped edges if you've got the patience.

For list of ready-made curtain manufacturers, send SAE to the GOOD HOUSEKEEPING INSTITUTE, Chestergate House, Vauxhall Bridge Road, London SW1. People who'll make up curtains (and pelmets if required) from your own fabric include: FIONA

CAMPBELL, 255a New Kings Road, London SW6 (who provides a country-wide service); JEAN DUBASH OF LONDON, 453 Fulham Road, London SW10. For curtain trimmings try: LUTETIA, 38 New Cavendish Street, London W1; DISTINCTIVE TRIMMINGS, Kensington Church Street, London W8; ELIZABETH EATON, 25a Basil Street, London SW3. Also, haberdashery departments of big stores; in London, BOURNE & HOLLINGSWORTH, Oxford Street, W1, for instance, have a good selection.

3 For details of solid wood and brass poles (with endless permutations of pineapple/ fleur-de-lys finials), write to: COPE & TIMMINS LTD, Angel Road Works, Rego Estate, Angel Road, Edmonton, London N18 and W. A. HUDSON LTD, 115 Curtain Road, London EC2. Also for elegant tie-backs, and coronas if you want to drape curtains over a bed-head. For internally corded and adjustable poles, write to KIRSCH, see 1. For cheap but convincing plastic-finished poles and finials, try W. A. HUDSON's *Rolls Regency* pole. Or buy a brass rod and rings from an ironmonger, and add hollow brass ball ends (much cheaper than solid) and brass brackets from a specialist shop like J. D. BEARDMORE, 3–5 Percy Street, London W1. If you've cut scallops from a non-fray fabric like PVC or felt, punch in brass eyelets with a Jones eyelet kit for a professional look, and use split brass rings.

4 You can buy spring roller kits from: WILLIAM WHITELEY, Queensway, Bayswater, London W2 and G. F. F. BARTLETT & SONS, 450 Edgeware Road, London W2.

5 Big stores like HARROD's and WHITELEY's are usually prepared to make up roller blinds from supplied fabric. Small specialist shops include: DE WINTER, 233 Kensington Church Street, London W8, who runs a country-wide postal service, and PETER WARD, Studio House, Blackheath Village, London SE13.

6 For details of made-to-order roller blinds in manufacturer's fabrics:

Sunlover	South Wales Blind Co
William O'Hanlon & Co	Llwynypia
49 Dale Street	Tonypandy
Manchester M60	Glamorgan
Sunstor Blinds	Sunway Colourwave Blinds
G. Hall & Co	Venetian Vogue Ltd
Fitzherbert Road	Bath Road
Farlington	Slough
Portsmouth	Bucks
Hants	

7 For details of made-to-order Venetian blinds:

Faber Ltd	Sunway, Venetian Vogue Ltd (see **6**)
Viking House	
Kangley Bridge Road	
Sydenham, London SE26	
Luraflex	Ventolux
Hunter Douglas Ltd	Ventolite Venetian Blinds Ltd
Wellington House	Kettering Road North
New Zealand Avenue	Boothville
Walton-on-Thames	Northants
Surrey	

For wooden-slatted Venetian blinds: TIDMARSH & SON, 1 Laycock Road, London N1.
8 For details of vertical blinds: FABER (see **7**); *Louvredrape*, VENETIAN VOGUE LTD (see **6**).

139

9 For details of pleated paper blinds: Sampson Pleatex, T. F. SAMPSON LTD, Creeting Street, Stowmarket, Suffolk (or more simply, visit your local branch of HABITAT). *Sampson Pleatex* comes in six colours, and can be screen-printed to order. Also: BALASTORE BLINDS, Baco Products, 250 Kingsbury Road, London NW9 (blinds come in cream only).

10 For details of plastic-reeded roll-up blinds: SUNDECOR BLINDS, Baco Products (as above); DUNBEE BLINDS, 117–123 Great Portland Street, London W1. Also ask at your nearest big Woolworth for their version. For pinoleum roll-up blinds, write to WILLIAM O'HANLON LTD (see **6**).

Usful address

The British Blind and Shutter Association
19 Leicester Square
London WC2

7 HANDLING PATTERN

1 Sanderson's *Triad* range is available from ARTHUR SANDERSON & SONS, 52 Berners Street, London W1, and if you write, they'll give you your nearest stockist. Also look out for Sanderson shops-within-shops at: HORROCKS's, Ridgway Gates, Knowsley Street, Bolton; SCHOFIELDS, The Headrow and Lands Lane, Leeds 1; W. ROWNTREE & SONS, 31–39 Westborough, Scarborough; and far too many others to list.

Sanderson aren't the only people who have wallpapers with matching fabrics. COLES, at 18 Mortimer Street, London W1, stock beautiful but more expensive French papers, often with matching fabrics and matching borders. ELIZABETH EATON, at 25a Basil Street, London SW3, stocks a wide range of imported papers, sometimes with matching fabrics.

Other wallpaper suppliers worth contacting for stockists: E. N. HEATH, Thames Road, Crayford, Kent, who import Rasch wallpapers with deliciously pretty Victorian patterns; EDGAR BROTHERS, 17a Curzon Street, London SW3, who import fabulous American papers (and fabrics); OSBORNE & LITTLE, 262a Brompton Road, London SW3, who print Gothic and Chinoiserie papers to order, and have hand-painted papers by leading designers.

SANDERSON, CROWN and COLES include patterned vinyl wall coverings in their range. Other ranges worth watching: ICI's *Vymura* range (stockists from Vymura, ICI House, Millbank, London SW1), and NAIRN COATED PRODUCTS' *Kingfisher Vinyl* (stockists from Nairn Coated Products, 6 Cranford Way, London N8).

1a Wallpaper terms

'Smearproof' or 'spongeable' merely mean that fast inks have been used in the printing, not that any protective coat's been added. All standard machine-printed British wallpapers *have* to use fast inks, so the terms are only worth looking for with imported or hand-printed papers.

'Washable' means that a fine protective coat has been added, but it *is* only fine, so don't try more than a gentle dabbing with a soapy (don't use detergent) sponge. The main advantage lies not so much in dirt-resistance as steam-resistance; in a kitchen or bathroom, steam can seep through a standard paper and cause peeling and discoloration.

'Scrubable' wallpapers aren't really papers at all. They're sheets of vinyl that are bonded to a paper backing so you can stick them up. And you can literally scrub, even with an abrasive cleaner if you're faced with a really stubborn stain.

140

1b Wallpaper sizes

A British roll, sometimes called a 'piece', measures 11 yds long by 22 in. wide, and most continental papers measure the same (though check before buying). This includes $\frac{1}{2}$ in.-margins on either side of the roll. Unless the paper's 21 in. wide and ready-trimmed, ask for trimming to be done at the shop, or you'll spend hours with a pair of scissors and days nursing the blisters. Vinyl wall-coverings are tough enough not to need protective margins in the first place, and British rolls always come 21 in. wide.

Estimating quantities

For British and most continental papers, the table below, reproduced by courtesy of Wallpaper Manufacturers, gives a rough guide as to how many rolls you will need for your room. Obviously it is only rough, because it cannot take into account individual numbers and sizes of doors and windows. Nor can it allow extra if your paper has a large pattern, known in the trade as a repeat, that will involve a lot of wastage. Sometimes the saving on doors and windows evens out the extra needed by a large pattern but when in doubt your retailer should be able to help you.

WALLPAPER CALCULATION TABLE

Height in feet from skirting	Distance around room in feet																	
	30	34	38	42	46	50	54	58	62	66	70	74	78	82	86	90	94	98
7 and under $7\frac{1}{2}$	4	5	5	6	6	7	7	8	8	9	9	10	10	11	12	12	13	13
$7\frac{1}{2}$ and under 8	5	5	6	6	7	7	8	8	9	9	10	10	11	11	12	13	13	14
8 and under $8\frac{1}{2}$	5	5	6	7	7	8	9	9	10	10	11	12	12	13	14	14	15	15
$8\frac{1}{2}$ and under 9	5	5	6	7	7	8	9	9	10	10	11	12	12	13	14	14	15	15
9 and under $9\frac{1}{2}$	6	6	7	7	8	9	9	10	10	11	12	12	13	14	14	15	15	16
$9\frac{1}{2}$ and under 10	6	6	7	8	8	9	10	10	11	12	12	13	14	14	15	16	16	17
10 and under $10\frac{1}{2}$	6	7	8	8	9	10	10	11	12	13	13	14	15	16	16	17	18	19

Number of rolls required

2 Good co-ordinated ranges as far as bed linen and towels go are made by CHRISTY's (write to W. M. CHRISTY & SONS, 15 Cavendish Place, London W1 for stockists); and OSMAN (write to OSMAN TEXTILES, 18 Noel Street, London W1). MARKS & SPENCER have started co-ordinating some of their bed linens, and very good they a.e too.

3 If you can't find the patterned carpet you like, and are feeling *very* affluent, the following people design and make carpets to order: A. R. D'ALBRIZZI, 1 Sloane Square, London SW1; DAVID HICKS, 23 St Leonards Terrace, London SW3; and WILLIAM MCCARTY, 14 Manson Mews, London SW7.

8 CHOOSING THE FURNITURE

1 Some good places to look for modern furniture

ALBRIZZI DESIGNS, 1 Sloane Square, London SW1 (cool, sophisticated and *expensive* perspex, glass and chrome-steel furniture); ARAM DESIGNS, 57 King's Road, London SW3 (expensive again, but superb furniture and lighting, some Aram's own, some from the Continent); DAVID BISHOP, 289 Kings Road, London SW3; FORM INTERNATIONAL,

Avon Trading Estate, Avonmore Road, London W14 (makers of many modern classics—see pages 62 and 63). HABITAT, 156 Tottenham Court Road, London W1 and 206 King's Road, London SW3 (mostly Conran, but some classics, and continental furniture; for branches outside London, see*); HEAL & SON, Tottenham Court Road, London W1 (most comprehensive selection of modern furniture in London); JOHN BOWLES & CO., 143 North Street, Brighton (part of Heal's); OSCAR WOOLLENS, 421 Finchley Road, London NW3 (often the first with exciting continental designs); ZARACH, 183 Sloane Street, London SW1 (similar range to ALBRIZZI).

*Habitat, regional branches:

14 John Dalton Street
Manchester

Birmingham Centre
New Street
Birmingham

Haymarket Centre
Leicester

144–147 Victoria Centre
Nottingham

Clifton Heights
Triangle West
Bristol

108 The Promenade
Cheltenham

11 Churchill Square
Western Road
Brighton

14–16 Eden Walk
Kingston, Surrey

1111–14 The Whitgift Centre
Croydon, Surrey

4 North Street
Guildford, Surrey

12 Westmoreland Place
Bromley, Kent

18 Queen's Road
Watford, Herts

Direct or mail order

Write off for catalogues to: DAVID BAGOTT, 266 Old Brompton Road, London SW5 (chunky pine and foam furniture; cheap, but not always well-finished); DESIGNSTORE, 10 Lauderdale Parade, London W9 (tubular-steel frame furniture, good finish and colours); HABITAT BY POST, Hithercroft Road, Wallingford, Berks (comprehensive and excellent mail order range); HULL TRADERS, 7 Sedley Place, Woodstock Street, London W1 (painted fibreboard *Tomotom* range—cheap and cheerful in the best sense); NEW DIMENSION, Manor Road, West Ealing, London W13; 1a Church Road, West Croydon, Surrey, and 53 Essex Road, Islington, London N1; 74 London Road, Riverhead, Sevenoaks, Kent; Tamworth Road, Measham, Leics. for buying direct. Mail order from NEW DIMENSION, Manor Road, West Ealing, London W13 (good design and terrific value—treading hard on HABITAT's heels); MARTIN SYLVESTER, Little Clarendon Street, Oxford (colourfully-stained furniture).

Modern furniture by mail order only

PACE FURNITURE, Bell Street Mews, Ravenscroft Road, Henley, Oxon (wide and excellent range); PIRA, 10 Hoxton Square, London N1 (beech and canvas safari chairs); TOTUM, 19 Bruton Place, London W1 (good quality range); SIGNALS DESIGN, 52 Esplanade, Poole, Dorset (cheap but expensive-looking unit seating—pine with squidgy button-backed cushions).

2 Never rely on a feeling for size—this is something that invites disaster. Very few people can look at a space and gauge how big it is, so measure it before you go shopping —and take a steel measure with you in case you see something you like, to save waiting about for an assistant to tell you its dimensions. If you're buying, or intend to buy several items, it's a good idea to make a floor plan and cut out scaled-down furniture shapes from paper, so you can see if they fit.

Making a floor plan

Mark off a large sheet of paper in 1-in. grids; each square represents 1 sq ft of floor space. Of course, you have to make the measurements carefully—a minor mistake could make all the difference between a sofa fitting perfectly between two military chests or being too big to slip between them. Remember to draw in all the doors, windows and chimney breasts—also the electric power points, because you may want to put certain items of furniture near them.

Next make your furniture templates, using the same 1 sq ft to 1 sq in. scale. Then all you have to do is arrange them (much easier than pushing the real things round the floor), making sure you leave plenty of room for ventilation and traffic lanes. It may seem a bit of a fiddle at the time, but it could save you plenty of heartaches later.

3 Good places for junk

Junk Cities: you'll find them in London at 67 Bell Street, NW1; 45 Crawford Place, W1; North End Road, W14; King's Road, SW10, and just a bit farther up in New King's Road. Also try THE SALVATION ARMY, early Saturday mornings at 124 Spa Road, Bermondsey, London SE16; AUSTINS of Peckham, London SE15; SIMMONDS, 180 North Gower Street, London NW1. And obviously, wherever you live, visit your local sale rooms (BONHAM's, at 75 Burnaby Street, London SW10 often have extra-cheap auction buys). Jumble sales are worth a visit, particularly if you are furnishing from scratch. Other people's cast-offs—especially in areas where taste hasn't caught up with current trends—can yield treasures, viewed with a discerning eye.

4 If you can't find what you want in dress fabric departments, LIBERTY's (Regent Street, London W1) has a small but superb range of PVC-treated furnishing fabrics. Branches of HABITAT sell plain and patterned PVC-treated furnishing fabric in good colours.

5 Best range of felts (every shade in widths up to 72 in., can be found at B. BROWN LTD, 32–33 Greville Street, London EC1. Samples sent on request. Meantime, JASPER KNIGHT INTERIORS, at 8 Danbury Street, London N1 keeps a good selection of felts with matching paints.

PS on hessian: Super cheap fabric for curtains. Find it at B. BROWN LTD; at RUSSELL & CHAPPLE, 23 Monmouth Street, London WC2 (who also stock inexpensive jute and canvas); and at JOHN OLIVER, 33 Pembridge Road, Notting Hill Gate, London W11 (like his felt, this can be specially dyed to match his own vibrant paint colours). For using felt and hessians as wall coverings, *12.6.

9 A PLACE FOR EVERYTHING

There's no shortage of good storage systems on the market (though there may be a shortage of money when you find out the prices). Some of the best-looking, most efficient and most expensive are by: STAG, Haydn Road, Nottingham and PROGRAM MEREDEW, Dunhams Lane, Letchworth, Herts. Cheaper version is by LIMELIGHT, North End Road, Wembley, Middlesex, and excellent-for-money versions come from

NEW DIMENSION (for addresses, see 8.1) either direct or mail order. Even cheaper version is available mail order from KEWLOX (Products) Ltd, Belcon Industrial Estate, Essex Road, Hoddesdon, Herts; equally cheap is the *Lundia* range of whitewood components from REMPLOY, 415 Edgware Road, London NW2.

Worth a special mention: CUBESTORE at 62 Pembroke Road, London W8, who make reasonably inexpensive and extremely handsome knockdown storage, in wood or hardboard; RT DISPLAY SYSTEMS, at 1 Chelsea Manor Studios, Flood Street, London SW3, who make clear glass storage; GRATNELL FITTINGS, at 256 Church Road, Leyton, London E10, who make clear perspex or white plastic drawers and trays, and metal uprights, so you can fit out a wardrobe or wardrobe alcove; ADD-A-DRAWER at 4 Anerley Station Road, London SE20, who make plastic drawers that you can build up, or simply hang beneath a worktop.

10 ADDING THE ETCETERAS

1 The best places to find posters are: GALLERY FIVE, 14 Ogle Street, London W1; POSTER BY POST, 43 Camden Passage, London N1; and of course, the LONDON TRANSPORT Publicity Poster Shop, 280 Old Marylebone Road, London NW1. All of these sell mail order as well as direct.

2 If you want something simpler, clip your print between a piece of cut-to-size hardboard and $\frac{1}{8}$-in. thick Perspex with neat chrome-finished EMO clips. Cut-to-size Perspex is available from G. H. Bloore, 68 Willow Walk, London SE1. EMO clips from: Paperchase, 216 Tottenham Court Road, London W1.

11 HALLS THAT SAY WELCOME

1 Mirrors can make a hall look lighter and brighter, and they needn't be expensive. Wooden-framed junk shop mirrors are still cheap, and make a terrific focal point tightly grouped on one wall. Or just one or two of them look good mixed with a group of paintings or prints. And even if a mirror is speckled with age around the edges, you can remove the frame, and replace it with a speckle-hiding hardboard cut-out. This can be any shape you fancy—and you can paint it to match your colour scheme.

Mirra Tiles are cheap for the amount of impact they can have. A tight-knit group of varying sizes can look cool and sophisticated and bounce back as much light as one big and expensive mirror. They come with self-adhesive pads attached (you simply tear the protective paper off the pads and stick them up—making sure to get them straight *first* time, because you won't get a second chance). Available from most stores, builders' merchants and DIY shops throughout the country, they're made by S. GREENMAN LTD, 5 Singer Street, London EC2.

If your hall's so gloomy it needs several square yards of mirror to lighten it, consider *Melinex*, a kind of stiff, plastic silver foil, that comes by the yard, 2 ft wide, and costs only about 15p. You can fix it straight on the wall with double-sided *Sellotape*, but for a really good reflection, it's best stretched over a frame to make a smooth panel. Available in silver, gold, purple, pink, blue, red or green, it comes from PAPERCHASE, 216 Tottenham Court Road, London W1. For details of *Mirrolite*, *17.8.

2 It's all very well talking about 'plain' tiles, but the vast majority of them come fussily flecked or marbled to disguise dirt. AMTICO (stockists from Amtico Flooring, 22 Hanover Square, London W1), have always made perfectly plain tiles, but in solid vinyl they've been horribly expensive. Now GERFLEX (stockists from Gerland, 90 Crawford Street, London W1), have introduced a perfectly plain and much cheaper self-adhesive version. In 'Snow White' only, these tiles are great to look at—even if they do need seven dwarfs to keep them clean.

12 WHERE THE LIVING IS EASY

1 GOSLETT'S, who have stockists all over the country, make an excellent range of fire-places—everything from modern tile or stone to painted wood mantels with plaster mouldings. Write to Goslett's, 127 Charing Cross Road, London WC2 for stockists. Or if you want something exclusive, G. & A. BRYANT, at 46–52 Chapel Street, Luton, Bedfordshire, make modern and traditional fireplaces in everything from brick to marble, to order.

Modern fireplaces: Write to: BYRON FIREPLACES, at 193 Greenford Road, Green-ford, Middlesex and Quebec House, Richmond Road, Kingston-upon-Thames, Surrey. For modern stone fireplaces: MINSTER FIREPLACES, Minster Works, Ilminster, Somerset. For Danish free-standing fireplaces, write to: TASSO FIREPLACES, The Garden House, Lower Cookham Road, Maidenhead, Berkshire. For the hole-in-the-wall type fireplace, keep looking in magazines till you see exactly what you want, cut it out, and get estimates from local builders for making it.

Reproduction traditional: For faithfully reproduced traditional fireplaces (carved pine, etc), write to: HALLIDAY ANTIQUES, at Dorchester-on-Thames, Oxon, and at 28 Beauchamp Place, London SW3. For equally faithful but non-operational fireplaces, made in fibreglass and ready for painting, write to: VERINE PRODUCTS COMPANY, Folly Faunts House, Goldhanger, Malden, Essex.

Antique: For genuine old fireplaces, try J. CROTTY & SON at 74 New King's Road, London SW6 and 1 Tasso Yard, London SW6; CROWTHER & SONS, Syon Lodge, Isleworth, Middlesex; and HALLIDAY ANTIQUES, Dorchester-on-Thames, Oxon. Also try demolition contractors and any antique shop you happen to be passing. Finally, of course, keep your eyes open for any house that's being demolished or converted. Many beautiful old fireplaces simply get a hammer put through them. They *are* difficult to get out intact, but if you slip the foreman something, he'll have a damned good try at managing it.

Summery treatment for a fireplace

You can turn a summer-time fireplace into a worthy focal point: if you fill it with green leafy pot plants and cluster more plants thickly in the hearth, so the area becomes an indoor 'conservatory'; or clean the grate out thoroughly and pile it to the top with plain but brilliant-coloured Christmas baubles, chosen to complement your colour scheme. If your mantel's wooden, pinch an idea from David Hicks (no less), and make a chain 'curtain' by screwing tiny hooks into the mantel at 1 in. intervals, and hanging floor-lengths of Woolworth's lavatory chain from them. Finally for evening, mass thick and thin candles of varying heights together, and bask in the candle-glow. (On second thoughts, as candles are expensive, better save lighting them for when you're entertaining.)

2 Lighting by major manufacturers like ATLAS, ROTAFLEX, LUMITRON and MERCHANT ADVENTURERS is available from most department stores and electrical shops, and though they won't stock the full ranges, they should have catalogues you can order from. Try BRITISH HOME STORES for cheap and surprisingly well-designed lighting. For imported lighting (and sad to say, the best designs still come from places like Italy), try HEAL & SONS, Tottenham Court Road, London W1, and JOHN BOWLES & COMPANY (which is part of Heal's), at 143 North Street, Brighton. Also the various branches of HABITAT (for full list of addresses, *8.1).

Smaller shops that specialise in lighting include: for modern fittings, DAVID BISHOP, 289 King's Road, London SW3; STUDIO 1, 10 Stafford Street, Edinburgh. For traditional fittings, it's worth making a pilgrimage to CHRISTOPHER WRAY'S Lighting

Emporium, at 604 King's Road, London SW6. This shop's a veritable Aladdin's Cave of Victorian, Edwardian and 1920s fittings—and you can buy glass shades separately if you need replacements.

3 THE BRITISH CARPET CENTRE, at 14 Lower Regent Street, London SW1, gives advice and information on, *but doesn't sell*, the Axminsters and Wiltons of the 30-odd manufacturers it represents. It *doesn't* deal with tufted carpets—a marked disadvantage this, when tufteds are what most people buy. The main advantage is that you see the full ranges of the manufacturers that *are* represented in rug-size samples, so you get a very good idea of what they'll look like down. Other advantage is the BCC label, which helps you choose the right carpet for the right room by grading the carpets as follows: 'light domestic use', for example in bedrooms; 'light to medium domestic use', for example in dining rooms or studies; 'medium domestic or light contract use' (contract meaning for offices, hotels, or restaurants), for the same; 'heavy domestic or medium contract use', for example in halls and living rooms; and 'luxury domestic or heavy contract use', for these same rooms, if you've got the money.

THE PLAIN CARPET LIBRARY, at 58–60 Cannon Street, London EC4, has the largest selection of *plain* carpets for sale in the country, and also runs a postal service. Send a piece of fabric or wallpaper, state what room it's for, and they'll send suitable cuttings.

Inexpensive carpeting: SAPPHIRE CARPETS, at Lancaster Road, Ealing Broadway, London W5, stock discontinued lines and used exhibition carpet and coconut matting. The best time to visit is after an event such as the Ideal Home Exhibition, when stocks are high, but prices start from a low 50p per sq. yd. For 20–30 per cent reductions on branded carpets (thanks to bulk-buying policies), try: THE DODSON BULL CARPET COMPANY, 2–4 Little Britain, London EC1; and MILLER's, 14 Berners Street, London W1.

PS on buying carpets

Don't be misled by the names Wilton and Axminster. They simply refer to the way the carpets have been made—they're no guarantee of quality, which is determined by the strength of the fibre and the quantity used per sq. in. Wiltons and Axminsters are woven on looms, with the pile and backing made at the same time. Tufted carpets, however, are made of short lengths of fibre slotted into a ready-made backing and stuck into position with an adhesive. If you choose a patterned carpet, you'll probably find it's an Axminster, because this method of manufacture gives most scope for mixing colours.

As regards fibres, wool is the traditional carpet fibre and nobody's invented anything to beat it yet. But it is expensive. A practical compromise is to pick a carpet that's 80 per cent wool and 20 per cent nylon. This brings down the price slightly, and the nylon adds extra toughness.

Acrylic fibre (*Acrilan* or *Courtelle*) is the nearest synthetic to wool, because it's warm and springy—but alas, it's also expensive. Nylon is cheaper, but although virtually indestructible, it's hard and flat, looks slightly shiny, and has an irritating tendency to cling to your feet as you walk. Rayon is the cheapest carpet fibre and if used 100 per cent, it's utterly flat and dead to walk on—and also hell to vacuum because fluff *won't* pick up. However, blended with other fibres, it makes good but medium-priced carpets possible. All in all, you only get what you pay for.

4 For some funny reason, builders' merchants rarely stock cork tiles. If you're having difficulty finding them, write for stockists to: THE ARMSTRONG CORK COMPANY, Bush House, Aldwych, London WC2 (tiles are available sealed or unsealed, and in floor and wall tile thicknesses); WICANDERS, Maxwell Way, Crawley, Sussex (available vinyl-topped in natural, and several brilliant colours). Or, cut out the middle-man and order from DIRECT CORK SUPPLIES, 92a Earl's Court Road, London SW5 (wall cork available in rolls, floor cork in sheets or tiles).

5 Most magazines write blithely about 'simply sanding and sealing the floorboards', but there's nothing simple about it. Before you hire a sanding machine, be warned that it's hard, noisy and dusty work; that unless you've spent anything up to a day pulling out or hammering in protruding nails, the sandpaper rips to shreds; that the sander won't go into corners, so you'll have to grind away at them by hand.

If that hasn't put you off, sanders can be hired from: ENGLISH ABRASIVES (PORTSMOUTH) LTD, Nufloor, Rodney Road, Portsmouth (write to them for nearest hirer—it's a countrywide service); FLOOR RENOVATIONS, 34–36 Lauriston Road, London E9 (available in London area only); HIRE SERVICE SHOPS, Essex Road, Acton, London W3 (sanders available at their Berkshire, Buckinghamshire, Hertfordshire, Surrey and Middlesex branches too).

If you *have* been put off, the following people will come and do the sanding for you: THE GRAND METROPOLITAN FLOORING COMPANY LTD, 73 Kinnerton Street, London SW1 (a countrywide service); CORNER FLOOR SURFACING, 139 Brighton Road, Surbiton, Surrey (available London and the South); STANDARD FLOORING COMPANY LTD, 6 South Hill Park, Hampstead, London NW3 (a countrywide service).

6 Felt makes a warm and surprisingly practical wall covering. The best way to hang it is to apply *Heavy Duty Polycell* or *Clam 143* to the wall, not the felt, and position immediately with overlapping joints, that you cut to butt joints once the felt has shrunk. (See *8.5 for where to get it.)

Ordinary hessian is equally warm and practical (again, see 8.5 for where to get it), and can be hung two ways. Either as felt (but don't get too heavy-handed or the weave will sag and stretch when wet), or by sticking or tacking it to wooden battens criss-crossing the walls. Easier but more expensive method is to hang a paper-backed hessian, and stick it to the wall as for felt, but without overlapping the joints. Paper-backed hessian comes in a wide range of light-fast colours, and if you can't find it (because it's sold by the yard instead of the roll, it often ends up in soft furnishing departments), write to: BOYLE & SONS, Clayton Wood Close, West Park Ring Road, Leeds 16, for stockists. Or alternatively, buy a specially treated and stiffened hessian, where you can apply *Heavy Duty Polycell* or *Clam 143* direct. For stockists of *Muraweave* and *Baseweave* (available with matching-coloured curtains), write to EDGAR BROTHERS, 17a Curzon Street, London W1. For stockists of *Canotex* (available in natural as well as colours, so you can overpaint it with emulsion if you want to), write to: SANDERSON's, 52 Berners Street, London W1, or buy from them direct.

Wall cork can be bought from the cork tile manufacturers mentioned in 12.4, or you can buy rolls of thin cork wall covering from Sanderson's. But for a *much* cheaper and even more attractive result, buy panels of deep, peat-coloured cork either from: THE CORK INSULATION & ASBESTOS COMPANY, 14 West Smithfield, London EC1; or Armagh Works, Tredegar Road, Bowes, London E5. This *is* purely decorative, however—it crumbles easily (a coat of clear lacquer would help) and shouldn't be subjected to too much wear and tear.

13 GOOD EATING PLACES

1 China should always be good enough to go on display, and it needn't be expensive. If you're on a rock-bottom budget, stick to one colour, and however you piece your 'service' together (from reject china shops, market stalls, junk shops or somebody's chuck-outs), it'll look reasonable. Best bet, though, is to stick to plain white. This always looks good, and gives you an opportunity to add a few magnificent patterned junk shop finds like those old oval meat dishes that are still around.

Good places for china: any big store at sale-time (they really do knock one third off normal prices); THE REJECT CHINA SHOP, 33 Beauchamp Place, London SW3; the Stoke area, where many potteries sell seconds that look perfect to the untrained eye. SPODE, ROYAL DOULTON and PORTMEIRION potteries are well worth a visit if you're passing. If you can possibly afford it, invest in bone china. Although it looks fine and delicate, it's *much* tougher than pottery, which chips easily.

14   KITCHENS UNLIMITED

1 If you want double-access, buy a peninsular unit that has doors opening both sides—into the kitchen and dining areas. But if you want a more friendly, relaxed look, improvise a peninsular unit with a pine table, a mahogany chest or sideboard—anything that suggests a division in a more mellow way. BETTY HOPE's SHOP at 19 Beauchamp Place, London SW3 specialises in old kitchen dressers, tables, chairs, cupboards; DUCAL's *Country Style* range provides the modern equivalent, with everything from refectory tables to Welsh dressers, all in knotty pine.

2 Useful gadget to have with your sink is a pull-out hot spray with brush attachment. Great for final rinsing or getting stubborn grease off plates. Details from JAMES BARWELL LTD, Great Hampton Street, Birmingham 18.

3 If you'd like impartial advice about dishwashers, write to: THE DISHWASHER DEVELOPMENT COUNCIL, 25 North Row, London W1. And for background information so you'll know what advice you want, ask for their *Facts About Dishwashers* leaflet.

4 Choose between continuous and batch-feed waste disposers. With the former, you keep dropping in the rubbish until it's all disappeared. With the latter—more expensive but safer—you put in a load, and have to place the sink plug in position before it will operate. Get this kind if there are small children around—and make sure the main controls are out of their reach.

5 64-dollar question is whether you want a chest or upright freezer. Uprights take up less floor space and food's as easily accessible as in a fridge. Chests are slightly cheaper and less expensive to run. Good if you intend to freeze masses of meat—the knobbly shapes prefer wide open spaces to shelves. But bad if you've got a weak back, because you have to bend right over. As regards size, allow 2 cu. ft per person plus one for luck. For more information, send 10p and large SAE to the GOOD HOUSE-KEEPING INSTITUTE, Chestergate House, Vauxhall Bridge Road, London SW1, and ask for their booklet, *Choosing and Using a Home Freezer*. You can also get information from THE FOOD FREEZER COMMITTEE, 25 North Row, London W1.

6 SOME KITCHEN UNITS—and where to see them

Trade name and firm **Ready-made units**	Ranges	Showroom

BEEKAY-BAUKNECHT
Beekay New Era Ltd, 82–106
Cricklewood Lane, London
NW2. 01-452 0165
	Werkform
	Stilform
	Stilform
	  De Luxe
	Stilform
	  Exclusive
		At Cricklewood Lane; and at
		Kitchen & Bathroom Centre,
		18 North Audley St,
		London W1.
		Write HO for appointed
		dealers' list.

BLUE GATE Blue Gate Products Ltd, Beautility Works, Kavanaghs Rd, Brentwood, Essex Brentwood 225233	*Cresta 600* *Cresta 500* *Cresta 21* *De Luxe*	At factory: *Cresta 500* also at all Habitat branches. *Free planning service*
CHRISTIEN SELL Christien Sell & Associates Ltd, 45 Camden Passage, London N1 01-226 1146	*Long Range*	45 Camden Passage. *Free planning service*
DR BECHER FITTED KITCHENS R. McEwan & Co., Duke St, Woking, Surrey Woking 2401	*Rena* *Donna Rena* *Rena* *De Luxe*	Duke St, Woking, Surrey.
EASICLENE Easiclene Domestic Equipment Ltd, Woden Rd, Wolverhampton Wolverhampton 24973	*Princess* *Duchess* *Coronet*	Temple St, Wolverhampton.
ELECTROLUX Electrolux Ltd, Oakley Rd, Luton, Beds. Luton 53255	*Scandinavia*	Can be seen at local retailers. Write for list to Electrolux Kitchen Furniture Division, Oakley Rd, Luton, Beds. *Free planning through retailers*
ELIZABETH ANN Elizabeth Ann Woodcraft Ltd, Rhyl, North Wales Rhyl 2341	*Snowdon* *Elizabeth Ann* *Calypso* *Sherewood*	No showroom but several stockists have show suites. *Planning service £1—* *refundable upon order*
ENGLISH ROSE English Rose Kitchens Ltd, Wharf St, Warwick. Warwick 44441	*L Range* *P Range* *Metric Range*	At Warwick; also at 'Kitchens' 18 Berners St, London W1; Building Centre, Store St, Tottenham Ct Rd, London WC1. *Free planning service*

149

Trade name and firm	Ranges	Showroom
GREENCRAFT Tom Green (Joinery) Ltd, Ingatestone, Essex Ingatestone 3070	Greencraft	At Ingatestone; also at Building Centre, Store St, Tottenham Ct Rd, London WC1. Free planning service
GROVEWOOD Grovewood Products Ltd, Tipton, Staffs. 021-557 4921	Daintymaid Compact Impact	At Tipton. Free planning service
HYGENA Hygena Ltd, PO Box 18, Liverpool 051-546 3501	System 70 2000	64 Grosvenor St, London W1. Planning service
KANDYA Kandya Ltd, 2 Ridgmount Pl, London WC1 01-637 1281	Continental 900 Range	Ridgmount Place. Retailers provide planning service
LEISURE Glynwed Steel Pressings, Leisure Pressings Div., Nottingham Rd, Long Eaton, Nottingham. Long Eaton 4141	Leisure Line Leisure Luxe	At Nottingham; also at 28 Brook St, London W1. Free planning service
MULTYFLEX Multyflex Units Ltd, Modular Works, Dafen, Llanelly, Carms. Llanelly 2201	Solid Timber range Diamond Galaxy International Continental	Multyflex Design & Display Centres at Llanelly; Elephant & Castle Shopping Centre, London SE1; Engineering & Building Centre, Broad St, Birmingham. Free planning service

NU-LYNE
Earnshaw Bros. & Booth Ltd,
PO Box 27, Central Mill,
Burnley, Lancs
Burnley 21391
	500 Standard
	  range
	M500 range
	Clevedon range
	  (Standard & M)
	Henley De Luxe
		At Burnley.
		Free planning service

PAUL W. H. Paul Ltd, Breaston, Derby Draycott 2581	Transatlantic	Longmoor Lane, Breaston, Derby. Free planning service
POGGENPOHL UK Concept International, 58 Coombe Rd, New Malden, Surrey 949 1272	Form 2000	At appointed stockists; list supplied from New Malden.

Trade name and firm	Ranges	Showroom
QUALCAST Qualcast (Fleetway) Ltd, Charlton Rd, Edmonton, London N9 01-804 5051	*Dorchester* *Adelphi* *Fiesta*	At Edmonton.
REMPLOY Remploy Ltd, 415 Edgware Rd, London NW2 01-452 8020	*Remploy Kitchen* *Unit Range*	22 Bruton St, Berkeley Sq, London W1; also in Birmingham; Bristol; Cardiff; Glasgow; Oldham (addresses from HO)
SCHREIBER Schreiber Furniture Ltd, Rye House, Hoddesdon, Herts. Hoddesdon 66401	*Schreiber* *Kitchen* *Furniture*	At appointed stockists; list supplied from Hoddesdon.
SIEMATIC Fowler Rd, Hainault Industrial Estate, Ilford, Essex 01-500 0202	*6006, 5005,* *4004, 3003,* *2002*	No showroom. At appointed stockists; list supplied from Hainault.
STONEHAM Stoneham & Son (Deptford) Ltd, Powerscroft Rd, Footscray, Sidcup, Kent. 01-300 8181	*Estate* *Design 80*	At Sidcup.
WHITELEAF Goodearl Risboro Ltd, Princes Risborough, Bucks. Princes Risborough 3311	*3000* *Chiltern*	Princes Risborough. *Planning help available from* *local suppliers*
WRIGHTON Wrighton International Furniture, Billet Rd, London E17 01-527 5521	*Californian 2* *International* *De Luxe*	3 Portman Sq, London W1. *Free planning service*

Whitewood units

LIDEN Liden Products (Whitewood) Ltd, Whitewood House, 227 Lea Bridge Rd, London E10 01-539 5500	*Newline* *Liden* *K Range* *M Range*	No showroom.

Trade name and firm	Ranges	Showroom
SOLENT Solent Whitewood Ltd, Bridport, Dorset. Bridport 2305	*Solent Whitewood*	No showroom. See at agents and stockists. *Planning advice obtainable through agents*

Knockdown, home-assembly units

CAPRI System Equipments Ltd, Lagoon Rd, Orpington, Kent. Orpington 26741	*Capri Assembly Units*	At Orpington.
GROVEWOOD (see p. 150)	*Impact ; Compact*	At Tipton. *Free planning*
HYGENA (see p. 150)	*Hygena QA*	64 Grosvenor St, London W1.
REMPLOY (see p. 151)	*Carriholme*	22 Bruton St, London W1.
SOLARBO Solarbo Fitments Ltd, PO Box 5, Commerce Way, Lancing, Sussex. Lancing 63451	*Doric Forum*	At Lancing; also at 453 Fulham Rd, London SW10; Building Centre, Store St, WC1. *Free planning service*

Kit units for home assembly

IDEAL KITCHENS Ideal Timber Products Ltd, Dumbarton, Scotland Dumbarton 3284	*Ideal Pacemaker Ideal Homemaker Trendsetter*	Ideal Timber Products Ltd, Broadmeadow Industrial Estate, Dumbarton. *Limited planning service—free*
PEERLESS PO Box No 5, Weaste Rd, Salford, Lancs 061 736 8041	*Peerless self- assembly*	8–9 Berkeley St, London W1. *Free planning service for visitors. No postal service*

Because of limited space, this is a selective list. If you can't find what you want, write for further information to GHI, Chestergate House, Vauxhall Bridge Rd, London SW1

Recommended reading for DIYs

For do-it-yourself from absolute scratch, consider buying *The Complete Do-It-Yourself Manual*, £5·50 including postage and packing from READER'S DIGEST Association Ltd, Old Bailey, London EC4, or £6·95 from bookshops. Packed with good projects, including several really superb kitchens.

7 Aga have achieved a notable compromise. Their 'old kitchen range' type cookers can now run off oil and gas as well as solid fuel—and they come in sizzling, paintbox colours.

8 You'll find an excellent selection of wall and floor tiles (some from big manufacturers, some from individual craftsmen, some with matching wallpaper, some DIY), at the TILE MART, 151–153 Great Portland Street, London W1. For Italian, Provençal and Moorish tiles, try DOMUS, 260 Brompton Road, London SW1. For Spanish tiles, CASA PUPO, 30a Pimlico Road, London SW1 (see list of regional branches*; also look out for their shops-within-shops). For handmade tiles, contact the CRAFT CENTRE, 43 Earlham Street, London WC2, who'll put you in touch with craftsman-designers all over the country. And for stainless steel tiles, write to the STAINLESS STEEL TILE COMPANY, 667 Earl Street, Sheffield 1.

*Caso Pupo, regional branches

Birmingham New Street Shopping Centre, Birmingham

240 Victoria Centre
Nottingham

3 Palace Court
Westover Road, Bournemouth

15 St George's Walk
Croydon, Surrey

8 Brighton Place
Brighton

24 Woolmead
East Street
Farnham, Surrey

99 Regent Street
Leamington Spa

9 Kitchen assessories

Elizabeth David
46 Bourne Street
London SW1

Merchant Chandler
72 New King's Road
London SW6

Cucina
4 Ladbroke Grove
London W11
   also:
8 Englands Lane
London NW3

Kitchen Range
10 William Street
Edinburgh 3

Serendipity
9 Guildhall Street
Bury St Edmunds

David Mellor, Ironmongers
4 Sloane Square
London SW1

Suffolk

Habitat (for list of branches, see 8.1)

15 AND SO TO BED

1 Back in the 15th century beds were enormous (the famous Bed of Ware could easily have slept ten in comfort). Not that the people were enormous—one look at suits of armour is enough to prove they were tiny compared to us welfare state-fed lot. We're taller and broader, so you'd think our beds would have expanded—but far from it. They've been visibly shrinking as bedrooms have got smaller.

Fortunately, the new metric bed sizes are slightly larger than the old imperial ones. Standard single size is now 100 cm by 200 cm (3 ft $3\frac{3}{8}$ in. by 6 ft $6\frac{3}{4}$ in.) and standard double size 150 cm by 200 cm (4 ft 11 in. by 6 ft $6\frac{3}{4}$ in.). Ideally, a bed should be 6 in. longer than its occupant, so if you're married to a six-foot-plus hunk, ring the NATIONAL BEDDING FEDERATION (see end of this section) for advice on where to get a bigger version.

Although big beds are the most comfortable, in a small bedroom you may have to settle for the smaller metric bed sizes. These are: small single size 90 cm by 190 cm (2 ft $11\frac{1}{2}$ in. by 6 ft $2\frac{2}{3}$ in.) and small double size 135 cm by 190 cm (4 ft 5 in. by 6 ft $2\frac{2}{3}$ in.).

Blankets and sheets

As you've probably guessed, bed linen and blanket manufacturers are dragging their heels over the new metric sizes. All you can do is calculate a size that allows about 10 in. 'tuck-in' all round the bed. The National Bedding Federation recommends the following blanket size for metric beds: standard single size 80 in. by 100 in., standard double size 100 in. by 108 in., small single size 70 in. by 100 in. and small double size 90 in. by 100 in. The British Standards recommendation for sheets is a bit on the skimpy side, but for what it's worth, here it is: standard single size 72 in. by 111 in., standard double size 100 in. by 117 in., small single size 70 in. by 108 in. and small double size 90 in. by 108 in. Fitted sheets (and you'll be lucky if you can find *anyone* manufacturing them metric bed size yet) make bed-making easier—but you can't swap top for bottom on wash days.

2 FIRA (The Furniture Industry Research Association of Maxwell Road, Stevenage, Herts if you have any queries), found that in higher income groups, women needed 100 in. of hanging space and men 58 in. They also found that several smallish drawers were more useful than a few large ones and recommended an 18 in. by 12 in. module.

3 With one exception (and we'll come to it later), it's best to spend as much as you can on your bed—buy a cheap one and you're likely to have to spend a fortune on an osteopath. If you're buying a base, choose between 'firm-edge' (cheaper, but good if you're given to sitting on the edge of your bed) or 'sprung-edge', which is more expensive. Never put a new mattress on a worn-out base, or you'll soon reduce it to the same condition.

Types of mattresses

Matresses fall into two camps: latex foam like DUNLOPILLO, where quality's dependent on the density of the foam and how much support it gives, and interior sprung mattresses. These have springs sandwiched between protective upholstery: either 'open', where lines of springs are connected by wire; or 'pocketed', where springs are compressed and inserted into individual calico pockets. The more springs the better the bed (price is always a fair indication). Pocketed springs are softer and therefore more expensive but even the *most* expensive mattress shouldn't be expected to last more than 15 years. By the way, if you've got a Jack Spratt situation where one of you likes a hard bed and the other prefers a softer one, go for a bed where two mattresses of different firmness can be zipped or clipped together.

Wooden base, foam top: What if you're hard-up, but don't want a sagging mattress that will weaken your spine? If you think you can get used to a firm bed (and any osteopath will tell you it's the best, back-wise), buy a bed with a wooden base and a foam mattress on top. David Bagott at 266 Old Brompton Road, London SW5 makes a very handsome but cheap pine-frame version (direct or mail order) in kit form.

Water beds: These are available from WESTERN WATER BEDS at 49 Maddox Street, London W1 and 281a Finchley Road, London NW3. Puncture outfits are supplied (!) but they're not recommended if you live in a flat-conversion, where the floor may not be capable of taking a ton-weight of water.

4 To avoid draughts, be sure you don't position the bedhead under a window or in direct line between door and window. And to avoid glare, don't have it facing a window.

Ideally, leave about 2 ft 4 in. at either side of a double bed so that you can make it without bumping into the wall or other furniture. And leave about 3 ft 3 in. clear in front of chests or wardrobe drawer units, so you can pull out the drawers *and* have room to stand in front of them.

5 GRANNY GOODS, 6 Grays Inn Road, London WC1 have superb handmade crocheted and patchwork bedspreads. All made to order—so write for a brochure. Branches of CASA PUPO (*14.8) make fringed Spanish tapestry bedspreads to match their flower-patterned rugs. Colours are rich and exotic. Equally exotic but much cheaper: Iraqui hand-embroidered bedspreads (no two alike), from DOMIDION, 350b King's Road, London SW3. And for a splash of Hollywood opulence (if you can stand it), HEAL's of Tottenham Court Road, London W1, have fur bedspreads made of coney. Best overall selection of bedspreads probably lives at JOHN LEWIS, Oxford Street, London W1. The most enterprising out-of-London bedroom shop is probably HANTONS, 60 North Street, Chichester; everything from tapestry bedspreads to cane bedside furniture.

6 STUART & CHUBB, at 10a West Halkin Street, London SW1 specialise in intricate cane furniture. Their cane bedheads are extremely appealing—so are the glass-topped cane bedside tables.

General information

For specific queries about beds, ring (or visit for take-home leaflets): the NATIONAL BEDDING FEDERATION, 251 Brompton Road, London SW3, telephone number 01-589 4888. For general information write (enclosing a stamped addressed foolscap envelope) asking for their free consumer leaflets. To see a vast range of what's available, visit the LONDON BEDDING CENTRE, 26 Sloane Street, London SW1, remembering that like many 'centres', basically it's only a shop.

16 GREAT TO GROW UP IN

1 Good places to buy nursery furniture are: the various branches of HABITAT (for addresses, see 8.1) who stock small rush-seated pine chairs, good storage and bunks; HEAL's of London and JOHN BOWLES of Brighton for storage, bunks, playboxes etc.— often Scandinavian, and very attractive in pale solid woods like beech; HAMLEYS of Regent Street, London W1, for conventional small-scale wooden desks, tables and chairs; HULL TRADERS, 7 Sedley Place, Woodstock Street, London W1, for brilliant-coloured and beautifully designed tables, chairs and storage made of *tough* painted fibreboard, also available mail order. And of course there is always whitewood from your local department store, that you can paint in bright colours.

2 'Moses' wicker baskets on stands are obtainable from HARRODS, Knightsbridge, London SW1; also (less expensively) from your local showroom of the ROYAL NATIONAL INSTITUTE FOR THE BLIND; for addresses write to Head Office, RNIB, 224 Great Portland Street, London W1.

17 MAKING A SPLASH

1 RENUBATH resurface worn basins and lavatories as well as baths. Their address is 596 Chiswick High Road, London W4.

2 One of the best places for package deals or anything to do with bathrooms is HUMPHERSON & CO LTD, 6–14 Holman Road, London SW11. They stock several makers' products as well as making their own. Their patterned sanitary ware is very appealing—not so exclusive as GODFREY BONSACK's, but just as pretty. They are also more hard-wearing (you can safely scrub round it with an abrasive cleaner, though strictly speaking, it's better not to use an abrasive cleaner on any bath) and much cheaper.

If you're looking for something sophisticated, IDEAL-STANDARD's new *Penthouse* suite in tan is very handsome, and reasonably priced. And if you're a purist looking for clean-cut perfection, ADAMSEZ' *Meridian 1* range in white is superb.

3 GODFREY BONSACK at 14 Mount Street, London W1 is where you'll find lush, Hollywood-style bathroom fittings. Everything from gold-plated dolphin taps and circular sunken baths to a shower that looks more like a chandelier. Good builders' merchant for a wider range of 'up-market' fittings (including old-fashioned wooden-seated WCS, which are making a comeback) is EVERED SUPPLIES, at 18 North Audley Street, London W1.

4 Of course, the advantage of Perspex is that it's so light. One man can carry a Perspex bath upstairs on his back like a turtle—quite a point if you're modernising your bathroom by yourself. Another advantage is that it's easy to shape and colour so that it comes in a wide and exciting range of designs. Any disadvantage (apart from the fact that it scratches easily) has yet to be proved; baths are expected to last a lifetime and some experts think Perspex baths will lose their shape and go soggy and dull-looking after about 20 years.

This probably explains why pressed steel baths (which, incidentally are the cheapest), are frequently used, even though more expensive cast-iron baths are better quality. This is because the iron holds vitreous enamel better than steel, so the surface is longer-lasting. Also because the colours can be more accurately matched to vitreous china basins and lavatories.

5 If there are old people or children in your family, choose a bath with a grab rail so that they can haul themselves out safely. And keep a non-slip mat in the bath permanently. Also consider a special bathroom lock that can be opened from the outside if anyone gets into difficulties. Finally, of course, choose a medicine cabinet made to the BSI Standard that children *can't* open.

6 If you need information on showers, write to or visit, THE SHOWER CENTRE, 138 Theobalds Road, London WC1, where there are experts to advise you, plenty of showers on display and even more take-away leaflets.

7 Worth a special mention: acrylic taps by OPELLA, that don't get piping hot like metal taps; and SHAVRIN-LEVATAPS (from 25 Hatton Garden, London EC1)—the first gold-plated plastic taps!

8 Condensation occurs when warm, steamy air hits a cold surface, and there's nothing colder than a conventional mirror. So why not try *Mirrorlite*, a non-shattering, light-weight plastic mirror that's heat-shrunk on to panels. It gives a first-class reflection—though it *does* scratch and it doesn't take kindly to a lighted cigarette end. Unless you have kids who scuff everything in sight, it would make a superb bath-panel in a tiny bathroom, and practically 'double' the floor area. Made by ULTRA-LITE PRODUCTS LTD, 61 Connaught Street, London W1.

18 FINALLY ON THE HOME FRONT

1 If you think the work's been badly done, taking the decorators to court could prove prohibitively expensive even if you win. Much better to get them in a position where they have to sue *you*. In other words, don't pay the bill, or only pay as much of it as you think they've earned. Of course, it's much better still if you give yourself a degree of protection in the first place by using someone who belongs to the National Federation of Master Painters and Decorators of England and Wales. Member-firms adhere to a recognised code of practice that guarantees quality workmanship; you can find out who they are by writing to the Federation at 6 Hayra Street, Harrogate.

2 Good places for both interior and exterior door furniture are: KNOBS & KNOCKERS, 65 Judd Street, London WC1; J. D. BEARDMORE LTD, 3–5 Percy Street, London W1 (this shop is really for the trade so dithering isn't welcome—but there's a stunning selection of knobs, knockers, finger-plates, escutcheons, intricate brass hinges etc); CHARLES HARDEN, 14 Chiltern Street, London W1; COMYN CHING, 15–21 Shelton Street, London

WC2; G. & S. ALLGOOD, 297 Euston Road, London NW1 (good on modern door furniture and they stock *Modric*). Some big stores hold a good range of door furniture — notably PETER JONES, Sloane Square, London SW1 and JOHN LEWIS, Oxford Street, London W1.

3 A cylinder mortice lock (about £8·50 including fitting) on front and back doors is an essential, because all it takes is a few seconds and a piece of plastic strip to slip a Yale lock. If you add window locks, too (from about £1·50 per window) that should be enough to make a burglar pass on and try farther up the road.

Fitting locks to internal doors is less advisable. Once a burglar's managed to get *in* to a house, the chances are he'll break down the doors at leisure and leave you with a hefty carpenter's bill to foot. And just to complete the security scene, CAMREX of Camrex House, PO Box 34, 3 Tathan Street, Sunderland, County Durham), make a special paint for drainpipes, that renders them difficult to climb. Now go and forget your door keys!

4 If you want a traditional panelled front door, visit your local builders' merchant, who should have most of the permutations possible. Or visit THE DOOR STORE, 61–63 Judd Street, London WC1, who stock both interior and exterior doors, including some with decorative fanlights.

Note: Cheapest way to get a handsome old door and/or handsome old door furniture is to hang around any house that's being demolished or converted. Just give the foreman a tip to cover their scrap value — and make sure you're strong enough to carry them away.

INDEX